STRUCTURE

The Master Key to KINGDOM SUCCESS

Bishop Finace Bush

Unless otherwise noted, Scripture quotations are taken from the KING JAMES VERSION (KJV) of the Holy Bible. Amplified quotations are indicated as (*AMP*). New Living Translation quotations are indicated as (NLT). All versions used by permission of the copyright owners.

Editorial and publishing assistance provided by:

Carmen Santos Monteiro, ghostwriter, editor, and author of "**Blood Stains:** *All in the Name of Love*," "*Side Gig*," and "*Crème and Sugar at Midnight*" (Carsamontel@gmail.com).

First-line editing to a portion of this book provided by: Mignon Spencer.

ISBN 978-1-329-51235-1

TABLE OF CONTENTS

Dedication and Acknowledgments

I dedicate this book to my lovely wife, Denise, who stands by my side and is truly a gifted helpmate and assistant. To my four special children working with us in ministry: Cattina, Teaya, Finace III, and Augustus. To my special grandchildren: Finace J. IV, Finace J. V, Jada, Joshua, Jaden and Jalayah. To my two sons-in-law who consider themselves my paternal sons and to my numerous spiritual sons and daughters; I dedicate this work to you.

A special thanks to the Crown Christian Church International family; local and abroad; to my covenant brothers and partners who share in this great mission to plant, establish, and expand the Kingdom of God. To my special friends and members who assisted with typing, copying, and a variety of other ways to prepare for publishing. A special thanks to the plethora of traditional, contemporary, and classical writers, along with the Holy Spirit, who shaped my beliefs and convictions over the last forty years. To the most dedicated, supporting, and loving parents for whom a young man could ask: My most consistent prayer was that God would allow me to complete a project that the two of you could be proud of because your sacrifices are limitless. You deserve a crown for a job well done in rearing your four children; I will love and honor you always. To Rhonda, Harold [Fat's] and Cheryl, may God continue to bless and prosper each of you. To my special teachers and mentors; Apostle Frederick K. C. Price, D.D., Dr. Myles Munroe, William Evans, Kenneth Hagin, and OG Mandino. To my dedicated and most admired spiritual coverings Dr. Creflo and Taffi Dollar. You provoke, inspire, and motivate me to strive for excellence in all I do. Your spiritual ambitions and Kingdom agenda for spreading the Gospel over the world challenges me to do likewise. Thanks for your many feats of inspirations. I extend my highest honor and most sincere thanks to my Father God, His Son, Jesus (my elder brother), and His precious Holy Spirit. You are responsible for inspiring this work through me. I thank you eternally.

The PROFIT of the Earth is for ALL!

(Ecclesiastes 5:9)

Let's begin by acknowledging that the Holy writings indicate "The profit of the earth is for all" and is accessible to everyone who properly applies themselves to what the Creator left us. The impact of this verse should be felt immediately because it clarifies God's purpose for the earth's abundant supply of resources. If all things produced by the earth were distributed to all men equally there would be more than enough for everyone.

When we view this statement from a perspective of the inheritance God prepared for all humanity to enjoy, it exposes the fact that many diligent persons enjoy the comforts of earth because of their aggressive pursuit of a better tomorrow. While on the other hand, many slothful persons remain without earth's comforts because they are disoriented, dysfunctional, and disenfranchised.

Many people are bound to complacency through ignorance, which subjects them to a spirit of mediocrity. Wherever mediocrity exists the ability to accept non-progressive people and systems as they are will continue to erode that division of society and eventually prevail towards its non-existence.

On the other hand a hidden "profit" that earth affords everyone is realized when we use our earth time as a wise investment for eternity. This is the greater purpose that the Creator intended from the beginning. What we plant or sow in our earthly life will determine what we harvest or reap now and in eternity.

We must realize that there is more to life than what is going on here and now in the earth realm. We are a spirit that has a soul that lives in a body. Our body is not who we really are but is an earth-suit we wear while on Earth. This is so that we can exchange with earthly vessels like ourselves and all other forms of

Earth's habitation.

Keep this in mind, the Earth we live on is subject to a time-line, however, we are eternal creatures from a heavenly realm that uses our time to advance our eternal existence. Although the profitability of the earth is accessible to us, our most profitable endeavor on earth is to prepare ourselves for eternity.

Introduction

A significant book

I began this project with the assumption of the responsibility to motivate Believers to re-examine their lives through Scripture from the perspective of God's creative purpose for our existence. I had a burden and conviction that the Holy Spirit birthed in me through prayer, study, and observation of the conflict that Satan subtly plants both in the world and the church to divide and conquer.

There are many types of motivational and self-help books that assist secular society to succeed and are readily embraced by the religious community and viewed as effective tools for life. Yet, in many of the same religious circles, the words "**Christian success or prosperous Christians**" are viewed more negatively. This type of ignorance makes Kingdom bonding and Kingdom expansion difficult to realize.

The desire for exposing the Christian community to a combination of proven, practical truths, destroying myths, and heresies implanted by enemies of faith, is factored heavily throughout this work. Also, my desire to establish a clear pathway for Christian success through simple obedience to God's Word was equally important.

God wants each of His children to understand where and how they fit in His master plan. According to Genesis 1:26, we were created in the image and likeness of God, but we lost our true identity through Adam's sin. As we rediscover our identity through Christ, we are reconciled to our privileges and rights to operate as His sons.

Notice, John 1:12, *"But to as many as did receive Him, He gave the authority (power, privilege, and right) to become the children of God, that is, to those who believe in (adhere to, trust in, and rely on) His name—"* (AMP)

We must no longer continue to accept a lifestyle of defeat because we wear the badge of Christianity. Neither shall we stoop to poverty and depravity to suggest a false humility to a world that cannot comprehend spiritual truths. These grossly flawed perspectives are not acceptable nor do they represent our Father's will. They only serve the purpose of permeating the insignificant lifestyle of mediocrity that leaves most Believers without influence among their peers.

Notice the emphasis Jesus placed on the power and necessity of Heaven's influence in this world's system, as expressed in Matthew 5:13-16. *"You are the salt of the earth; but if the salt loses its flavor, how shall it be seasoned? It is then good for nothing but to be thrown out and trampled underfoot by men. You are the light of the world. A city that is set on a hill cannot be hidden. Nor do they light a lamp and put it under a basket, but on a lampstand, and it gives light to all who are in the house. Let your light so shine before men, that they may see your good works and glorify your Father in heaven."* (NKJV)

Clearly these statements from Jesus himself illustrates the need for Kingdom citizens to have primary influence, power, and authority in both the world's system and His Kingdom, so that every transaction in the earth realm is a reflection of Heaven.

In Paul's letter to the Colossians 4:5, 6, he compels the Believers in the same manner to, *"Walk in wisdom toward those who are outside, redeeming the time. Let your speech always be with grace, seasoned with salt, that you may know how you ought to answer each one."* (NKJV)

Also, Luke 2:52, states that, *"And Jesus increased in wisdom and stature, and in favour with God and man."* His growth in both realms which resulted in favor with both systems is evident in this passage and throughout the gospels, which illustrates the need to hold ourselves accountable to the demonstration of His example.

We have a great responsibility as Christians to win as many souls as we can for Christ. Therefore, each of us as Kingdom citizens have a personal duty to "ponder the path of our feet and let all our ways be established," (Proverbs 4:26). This is the surefire route to a successful, purposeful, prosperous, and fulfilling life of Christ-likeness or Kingdom influence.

The Master Key to Success consist of **scriptural disciplines** referred to as ingredients necessary for integrating the use of our efforts into one unified force that will make us consistently, effectively, and purposefully fulfilled each day.

Perhaps you lack a decisive internal core regarding your God-given purpose and personal mission, your occupation, role in society or how you relate to family, friends, and associates. Perhaps you have a good job but hate the work, or maybe you are someone who daily juggles a lot of things but don't derive any real joy or fulfillment from doing them.

It is time for us to realize that we were created from "God-stock" and "God-stock" is supremely victorious in *all* things. Understanding the power of transformation through mind renewal, using the Word of God, is the crucial link that adds the insight needed to balance our lives.

Notice how Ephesians 1:11, 12 expresses the fact that God makes all things correspond to His purpose *"according to **the counsel of His will'***, which demonstrates the decisive measure He uses to sustain the universal logic of all past, present, and future creations. *"In Him also we have obtained an inheritance, being predestined **according to the purpose** of Him who **worketh all things after the counsel of His own will:** That we should be to the praise of His glory, who first trusted in Christ."*

My aim is to convey the importance of everyone having an internal compass drafted from our understanding of God's purpose. Which supervises and directs our decisions, gifts, skills, relations, activities, and plans to ensure we live a wholesome life.

This will prevent us from becoming like cynics and skeptics who are miserable and cannot see above the logic that drives their lifestyle choices.

I am extremely excited for the readers of this book. I hope that my ten years of journaling and twenty-five years of principal insights will attract the masses of potential achievers who may have been deceived about God's true perspective of success.

As you read this book, I pray that you will keep an open mind, read prayerfully, reexamine the material against the Scriptures and allow the Spirit of God to confirm your way.

Chapter 1

The First Master Key

Correcting Your Foundation

Masonry is a popular home-building craft and has a remarkable durability that is appreciated when all the regulations and requirements for a particular structure are met. While few of us imagine that our homes will exist for centuries, when we choose masonry we're choosing a material that has precisely that capability.

Masonry is popular for many reasons, including its beauty, versatility and resistance to fire, earthquakes and sound transmission. Let's not forget masonry's remarkable durability that is appreciated when the requirements in a particular structure are met. While few of us think that our homes will exist for centuries, when we choose masonry, we choose building materials that has precisely that ability.

Some of the world's most vulnerable masonry structures are the Taj Mahal, the Egyptian Pyramids, the Coliseums in Rome, and the Great Sphinx of Giza have awed generations of people because of their ability to withstand time. Like masonry, the Holy Scriptures are more than able to make us wise. In conjunction with the Holy Spirit, Scriptures give us information and empowerment to work with, and make repairs to, personal areas of our lives; the kind of repairs that enable us to withstand normal tests and trials of life.

Notice, the words of Jesus, "*It is the Spirit that **gives life**, He is the life giver; the flesh conveys no benefit or profit at all. The **words** that I speak unto you **are spirit, and they are life**'*, John 6:63. Each of us should be concerned about whether we are building on the proper foundation by applying God's confirmable truths that give us the correct way to live.

A phrase that you will see repeated throughout these pages is found in Proverbs 16:25, "*There is a way that seems right to a man, but ends in multiple ways of death.*" Now let's begin this journey of reconstruction together.

Building on the Right Foundation

Notice the implication of Psalm 11:3, "*If the foundations are destroyed. What can the righteous do?*"

What is a foundation and why is it important to have one? Or, to make this more relevant; why do you do what you do and who or what influences the direction of your life? Are you living in a self-defeating cycle of frustration and chaos? Is it good to impress and appease others at the expense of your personal peace and power? Last but not least, who told you or what makes you think you've discovered the appropriate way to live?

Webster defines a "foundation" as the base on which something rest; or, the basis for which something exist; specifically the supporting part of a wall, house, relationship, system, reality, etc., and at least partially underground, the **fundamental principle on which something is founded**. It is the basis or standard; a supporting material or part beneath an outer part, as a foundational garment.

Greek nouns THEMELIOS or THEMELION denotes a thing, a standard, a principle or a system upon which something is built. It is used as a noun, with *lithos;* a stone. Herein lies the acid test to determine if our practices and habits are correctly established on the correct foundation.

If an action or reaction in which you engage constantly leaves you without internal peace or rest, you need to examine it or weigh it against the truth. What's happening to you may not be the problem, but how you handle it may be in need of change!

Many times we handle our affairs according to *what seems right to* us instead of what is appropriate [or the standard] for a situation. Here is something we should always remember; that which we consider *normal* usually determines the **importance** we place on it. Our definition of normalcy was probably shaped through the experiences of our developmental years, which may or may not have included God.

Things that are **important** to us are only important because they meet our *standards*; our *standards* impact and shape the perimeters [broad or narrow, right or wrong] of the way we believe and the things in which we believe. Our *beliefs* reside in our conscience which is the place where "strong-holds" are erected that form our deep-seated *convictions.*

Ultimately our *convictions,* referred to by Webster as "strong beliefs, or opinions", are the forces that work together to drive our *responses.*

This process influences our behaviors regardless of whether they are right or wrong. This is the single reason the standard for every operation needs to be tested against "truth."

If you are in any way like I was before I began this journey, testing your beliefs and practices against "truth" will divinely inspire you. You might see changes in your thought processes and habits that have developed over your life-span.

Whenever our convictions drive our responses, we are usually inflexible about the position we take whether it is correct or not. The problem is that we may have settled with the wrong frame of mind. The way we handle our personal issues and other people will, to a great extent, determine the quality and happiness of our lives.

This Brings Me To A Very Important Point

In Proverbs 4:26, we are advised to *"Ponder and consider well the path of our feet, and **let all of our ways** be established and ordered alright.* This passage suggests that there is an established route [foundational measure] for every way we might chose to take in this life. But in most cases we may not have "pondered and considered well...."

In other words we must act considerately in *all* we do by **"putting the word of God on one scale, and what we have done or what we are about to do on the other scale to see how they agree."** Be critical in examining if your way is good before God because this will determine whether it will end well. Do nothing rashly!

One reason Jesus commanded that we seek God's Kingdom and righteousness first is to help us weigh our actions and thoughts against the appropriate way [foundational measure] of fully living life. Note, *"But seek (aim at and strive after) first of all His kingdom and His righteousness (His way of doing and being right), and then all these things taken together will be given you besides."* (Matthew 6:33, AMP)

Another reason to seek the Kingdom is to prevent us from incurring God's wrath which shall be revealed against ALL ungodliness and unrighteousness.

We cannot pick and choose the part of righteousness we will prioritize, because God expects us to honor all of His sayings regardless of how it feels or what we think. Notice how the Apostle Paul addressed this issue to the Believers in Rome.

"For the wrath of God is revealed from Heaven against all *ungodliness* and *unrighteousness* of men, who hold the truth in unrighteousness, because what may be known of God is manifest in them, for God has shown *it* to them. For since the creation of the world His invisible *attributes* are clearly seen, being understood by the things that are made, *even* His eternal power and Godhead, so that they are without excuse.," (Romans 1:18-20)

It is Important to Know That Some Foundational Things Have Been Kept Secret

The secret things of God do not interfere with our ability to live successful lives. I'll discuss this thoroughly in chapter two.

Jesus stated in Matthew 13:35, "that it might be fulfilled which was spoken by the prophets, saying: *"I will open My mouth in parables; I will **utter things which have been kept secret** from the foundation of the world."* Isn't it interesting that God has kept some "foundational things" secret although they are the fundamental principles upon which activities both in Heaven and Earth rest?

Correcting Your Foundation

In Luke 6:48-49, notice how *The Message* Bible addresses the process of correction and the importance of a "right foundation". *"**If you work the words into your life**, you are like a smart carpenter who dug deep and laid the foundation of his house on bedrock. When the river burst its banks and crashed against the house, **nothing could shake it**, it was built to last.*

*But if you just use my words in Bible studies and **don't work them into your life**, you are like a dumb carpenter who built a house but skipped the foundation. When the swollen river came crashing in, **it collapsed** like a house of cards. It was a total loss."*

The *Amplified* further clarifies the need for right foundation using the same passages, *"For everyone who comes to Me and listens to My words [in order to heed their teaching] and does them, I will show you what he is like. He is like a man building a house, **who dug and went down deep** and laid a foundation upon the rock; and when a flood arose, the torrent broke against that house and **could not shake or move** it, because it had been securely built or founded on a rock.*

But he who merely **hears and does not practice** *doing My words is like a man who built a house on the ground without a foundation, against which the torrent burst, and immediately it collapsed and fell, and the breaking and* **ruin of that house was great.***"*

It is obvious from the focus of each version that when we fail to investigate the values, standards, and beliefs that govern our decision-making processes, our lives may be subject to collapse and ruin. Again, Proverbs 16, reads *"There is a way that seems right to a man,* [because it is most logical to him] *but the end there of are the ways of death."*

There are two general types of concrete failure which are also similar to our human experience: They are structural and surface. **Structural failure** usually results from outside forces like freezing water; and **Surface damage** most often is caused by improper finishing techniques or concrete mixtures that do not have the right ratio of something as simple as water to cement.

Until we are aware of the fact that our way of processing and determining is flawed and problematic, there is a possibility we will repeatedly make the same mistakes. Both structural [foundational] and surface [finishing] problems will continue to interfere with our ability to live a successful life with continuity.

Kingdom systems take an uncommon approach to power, peace, prosperity, and progress, because they are based on principles not practices. When we understand the principles, we can create effective practices. Notice how the wise man Solomon attempts to advance us through his insightful understanding of how a life should be properly set up.

Through skillful and godly **Wisdom** *is a house, a life, a home, or a family built, and by* **understanding** *it is established on a sound and good foundation, and by* **knowledge** *shall its chambers of every area be filled with all precious and pleasant riches. A wise man is strong and is better than a strong man and a man of knowledge increases and strengthens his power; For by wise counsel you can wage your war, and in an abundance of counselors there is* *victory and safety. **Wisdom** is too high for a fool: He opens not his mouth in the gate. **Proverbs 24:3-7***

I'm beginning with the last verse of this quote because it speaks directly to the description of a weak man who, for whatever reason, has decided to live as though wisdom is too high for him. He may not be aware of the daily cost to him resulting from his unchecked ways of assessing and evaluating his own practices against God's Word. His despairing way of thinking convinces him to refuse to take pains in the pursuit of the one resource without which God, His Creator, never attempted to accomplish anything. And that one thing is WISDOM.

So he sits down "***In the seat of the scornful,***" persecuting right methods and applications because of the blindness of his own heart. He foolishly remains content without wisdom, as though he has no capacity for it. Therefore the advantages he has for getting wisdom are all in vain to him.

His way is *"right in his own eyes"* without a confirmed alignment with truth; he is both judge and jury for those who differentiate from his course.

It is no easy thing to get wisdom but everyone must be willing to pay the price for it. Those of us who lead and are responsible for others in any capacity must use wisdom. It is a foolish thing when leaders are slothful and remiss in pursuit of the wisdom that corresponds with God's standards for living. So we are better equipped to lead others according to what is right by God's guidelines instead of our assumptions.

Assumption is not just the lowest form of knowledge it can also be the device of self-deceit that makes an individual vulnerable to wrong influences and positions with important people and issues. Both, Jeremiah and Paul, warned us to not be victimized by the deceitfulness of our own heart which can alienate an individual from God through shallow thinking and limited, untested imagination.

I speak not to fools and certainly you who are reading this material are not as fools who spend the quantity of their time in sport, entertainment, and pleasures more than in preparation for the service of your call and purpose.

I submit here that all leaders and young people should take pains to get wisdom so they may have a good reputation and be qualified for public business.

Note, when people neglect to prepare themselves properly for their own causes, that failure to prepare leaves a person unfit for service and ignorant of the measures necessary to advance causes, which councils or magistrates would heed.

Such a person will not be fit for representation because he would not have pursued that which is necessary to escape the deceitful experiences and shallow reasons of his own heart.

This is why King Solomon advised, saying, "*Get wisdom, get understanding: forget it not; neither decline from its words. Forsake her not, and she shall preserve you: Love her, and she shall keep you. **Wisdom** Is the principle thing; therefore get wisdom: and with all thy getting get **understanding**.*" (Proverbs 4:5-7)

Always remember that life does not yield wisdom just to reward our existence. Wisdom must be prioritized and pursued in order to obtain it.

Personal discovery through "Structure"

Over the course of my life, I have tried many concepts and strategies attempting to maximize my effectiveness. However, the one thing that continued to show up in my journals was a lack of continuity. Getting started had never been my problem. **Keeping momentum**, for lack of a better term, is the hurdle that kept me in bondage to mediocrity.

Like the Apostle Paul, "*to will was present with me, but how to perform I could not find.* I always had good intentions and urge to do, **but lacked the power** *(missing key)* **to carry it out.**" (Romans 7:18)

A revelation of myself that empowered my will

I was tired of not following through with many of the endeavors I would start. While praying in the Spirit one morning, a light turned on inside of me. The Holy Spirit began speaking about my need to develop a **spirit of persistence**. Apparently, at that time in my life, the focus of my goals was not adequate to sustain my endurance or drive.

I began examining my most passionate desires and narrowing my focus which enabled me to **define my purpose**. Laboring with my purpose enabled me to craft and **write out specific and clearly defined plans** which, in turn, strengthened my confidence. Sharing my excitement with others helped me realize the importance of **shielding myself from negative influences**. Then the Holy Spirit led me to **form covenant alliances** with persons willing to demand my accountability and encourage follow through.

The absence of this one quality kept me from accomplishing my goals. A few days later in a vision, God gave me a master key that enabled me to define myself, identify my purpose, establish an inner core of disciplines, and write a mission for my existence.

The Holy Spirit said "You lack structure!" That is the master key to your success.

Breaking deeply imbedded habits that caused me to procrastinate and give up on projects and tasks was very difficult for me initially. I would start strongly and passionately but **lose focus** because my most important actions did not correspond with my goals. My inability to **say no** and my **lack of commitment** to my own dreams made me a "sitting duck" for distractions from people who had **no value of time or goals for their future**. I did not know what to do to break this self-defeating cycle. While I was viewed as a helper to others, I would find myself in a crowd of people and feeling lonely because I was not being fulfilled.

So, one morning after my time of worship and praying in the spirit, I began meditating on 1Corinthians. 9:25-27 and Joshua 1:8. Finally, near the end of my devotion the Holy Spirit spoke to me saying, **"You lack structure! That is your missing ingredient and master key to success."**

Over the course of the next few days, I gave thought and study to what was revealed. It became obvious to me that I needed to **arrange important daily functions by prioritizing them to correspond with my goals.** As I prayed for wisdom, the Holy Spirit continued clarifying and translating my purpose into a plan of action.

With this new enlightenment I was beginning to see more clearly. Each day as the light became brighter I began receiving "structure" in the form of principles of discipline that constructed a clear pathway to a strong, effective, purposeful, well-balanced Christian life.

Throughout the first several weeks of visitations, the following eight disciplines were revealed to me in four categories: **Categories 1 and 2:** My **Time** needs an Assignment; My **Relationships** needs Defining, and **Categories 3 and 4:** My **Devotion** needs Persistence and My **Change** needs Insistence.

As I defined each key discipline, it became more obvious to me that the reason I constantly failed to accomplish my endeavors was due to a lack of structure. It also became clear to me why so many others who are highly gifted, talented, and scholastic have difficulty making their dreams become reality.

To live without structured priorities was disastrous for me. Each day, I began with the intentions of making my life better only to discover by the day's end that I had allowed another pearl to get away. Like so many others, **I would drift from day-to-day as if I had an agreement with time to wait on me. In the meantime, my foolish malpractices** and lack of adequate priorities left me continually empty and frustrated.

Like one of my favorite writers, Og Mandino, "Tomorrow I will begin, I told myself day-after-day. I didn't know then, that tomorrow is only found in the calendars of fools." Blind to my foolish faults, I was wasting my life in deliberation for I knew not what, and I would have procrastinated until it was too late had it not been for the Holy Spirit giving me these keys.

Make a daily planning log

The structure keys were first a daily planning log to manage my daily functions so that I could focus on increasing my effectiveness. Immediately, I began experiencing a more fulfilled life. As I became more conscious, I began to realize the amount of time I was wasting on sports programs and other insignificant activities that created added obstacles and distractions.

A New Spirit Started Developing in Me

A sense of "**Destiny**" had seemingly been imparted to me. I became hungry, alert, and conscious of my surroundings and the actions I needed to take in order to remain focused and persistent. I begin taking control of each day, without allowing changing situations and challenges to dominate me. This actually felt like being born again, again! Man, I was really alive again! I was revived and filled with vision and a clear mission.

I also had an abundance of energy and enthusiasm to accomplish my priorities. With this key I knew I was ready to conquer the world. Now I understand; now I get it.

Fresh Revelation is **Fresh** Anointing!

Fresh Anointing is **Fresh** Power!

Fresh Power is **Fresh** Ability; God's Grace!

The grace that accommodates the "Spirit of Revelation" is empowerment to accomplish and succeed in every endeavor inspired by God. This is an encouraging expression that echoes in my spirit each day I enter into my morning devotion.

I have always held the conviction that God never gives us **responsibility** without giving us the **ability [grace]** to carry it out. But, many times my personal struggles left me vulnerable to continual distractions that hindered me from the completion of important daily tasks.

My life had no significant structure to enable consistent effectiveness. I finally realized that life is a maze for anyone who cannot define their purpose and **lacks the discipline to prioritize.** While I appeared to be an accomplished pastor and professional artist, my identity crises subjected me to constant frustration and defeat.

As a leader I had to acknowledge that **attempting to reconstruct a life is a very difficult task or challenge.** I desperately needed to go through the process of gaining mastery over my personal struggles if I were to succeed in assisting others with their struggles.

Like the Apostle Paul, I had to learn how to; *"keep my body disciplined, to bring it into subjection: for fear that after proclaiming the things pertaining to the gospel to others. I myself should become unfit, not being able to stand the test, and be rejected as a counterfeit."*

Life's decisions are perplexed when one does not know where, or how to begin especially if the individual is unable to discern the most important step to take first. The wrong perspective of God, people and things, along with the absence of vision, purpose, and self-awareness might keep an individual stuck in a self-defeating cycle. This deceitful cycle consist of a pattern of thoughts and actions that continue to produce more of the pain and discomfort from which we may desire to be free.

Living daily like this can become difficult. In my case, for many years I was too stubborn to change, and I was addicted to doing things the same way in spite of my many failures. I had an **illusion of safety in familiarity**.

New Light!

Now life is being revealed to me in a new light. This new **revelation** started generating increased personal ability and power to accomplish my aspirations. Paul described this ability we receive from God as:

*"Precious treasure, the **divine light** of the Gospel that **we possess** in [our] earthen vessels that the excellence, exceeding greatness of the power may be shown to be **of God** and **not from ourselves**"* (2 Corinthians 4:7)

In other words, it's not by our strength or ability that we accomplish great things, but by God's Spirit. *"Not by might, nor by power, but by my Spirit, says the Lord of hosts."* (Zechariah 4:6)

Through this, my desire began to stimulate a sense of urgency and purpose within me. A new light was turned on inside of me that made me take responsibility for my successes and failures. This new light enabled me to understand that **the Word of God expresses two major categories of successful living**: 1. Success attained by striving to enter into a better and more abundant tomorrow. 2. Success attained by one's ability to accept things as they are without internal conflict or competing desires.

I will discuss these two ideas by using "categories" to make it easier to follow.

First, let's discuss category 1. The difference between those who are successful and those who are the failures in this group may be that the *successful persons keep applying themselves* even when the **risks** are high. They develop a routine through persistence that turns into momentum. They major in the **possibilities** not the risks. But, on the other hand, those who fail in this group usually stop applying themselves whenever **risks**

surface. They major in the **risk** instead of the possibilities

Misinterpretation of the Risk Factor

Many people fail to understand that **risk** actually **determines** the **value** a person places on a thing or the benefit of accomplishing a goal. The more value I place on the goal or the thing, the more I am willing to take the risk. The less value it holds, the less likely we are to take the risk.

Value-driven desire is the **fuel** to **persistence** that enables a person to hurdle over **risk** when it is part of the process. In some cases, it is not that people identified as failures are true to the definition of failure, but they simply fail to place value on the things they desire to accomplish due to fear of personal risk or failure.

So let's define **personal risk** as, *the things we don't want to be affected by processes that we are uncertain of because we never experienced them. Or, to have an abundance of uncertainty about the changes that may occur in personal relationships, financial stability, savings, diet, [eating habits], schedules, and many other things that rank high on a person's priority list.*

Here's an example, this can be **explained by comparing**; the woman with the issue of blood identified in Mark 5:25-28, with the young rich ruler mentioned in Matthew 19:16-22. The woman with the issue **valued** her **deliverance above** the **risk of losing** all she had, but the young rich ruler **valued** his personal **withholdings** above the **risk** of getting delivered, and experiencing fulfillment on God's terms.

Now let's look at Category 2: Success accomplished by one's ability to accept things as they are, without internal conflict or competing desires. This group can be divided into the **content** and the **miserable**.

The **Content**, are those who experience consistent internal peace that balances their **effort** with their **expectations** each day. They live within the comforts of their own conscience without competing desires despite daily challenges or exposure to better, more modern, or abundant things.

For them, *"godliness with contentment is a great gain."* They accept what they are given expecting no more or less and they are always content with such things as they have. **As it is written** in the epistle of Romans 14:22, *"Happy is he who does not condemn himself in what he approves."* **A few examples** are teenagers and adults who are not compelled to get a driver's license, move out on their own, buy a car, or pursue a career.

Now the **Miserable** in this category are not hard to identify because often their day ends without them being any closer to the change they desire to make, goals they want to accomplish, or finishing tasks they intended to complete.

Their **pretended contentment** is driven by the **fear of not being able** to compete, accomplish, or complete a task to some other person's satisfaction. Their fears and insecurities cause them to pretend to be content so they are not pressured to attempt something and fail. They are **afraid to fail** so they refuse to try.

I will further explore the word **"afraid"** and the primary "fears" we must master that I discuss in the upcoming chapter, "Mastering FEAR."

Daily thought and meditation

Fresh Revelation is **Fresh** Anointing!

Fresh Anointing is **Fresh** Power!

Fresh Power is **Fresh** Ability and God's Grace!

SUCCESS

One of the most important issues we will likely deal with in this lifetime is Success. The Holy Spirit once whispered to me that "many people are consumed with life but not learning how to live it." Although God has provided a door to life, many of His children still prefer to live by their own measures: guessing, experimenting, or simply following the way of the masses. All the while, they suffer great pain and agony at the hand of their own decisions.

The Holy Scriptures make it clear that *"The way of life is not in man"* despite how it appears from our own way of viewing things. When we attempt to exist in this life apart from God, our Creator, without His Word as our standard for living, every way is right in our own eyes. Solomon stated in Proverbs 3:7, *"Do not be wise in your own eyes; Fear the LORD and depart from evil."*

John 10:1-10 exposes Jesus as both the key and the combination to "True life." Clearly the solution is to enter in the right door. In John 8:12, Jesus reemphasized that *"He is the light which is life";* after He convicted the conscience of those who judged the woman found in adultery. These are only two of the many accounts that confirm John 1:4, which states that *"in Him was Life and the Life was the Light of men,"* which is to say the **light** [correct instructions for living] was in the **life** [Zoe, Greek.for the God kind of life]. In other words, the proper way to live is in the principles Jesus subjected His life to because "the life was in the light" and not in the way of the "thief"; trickery.

"Salvation the true foundation of Life"

In the Gospel of Matthew 7:21-27, Jesus taught an important lesson regarding the single most important priority in life.

Although society may have decided that the practice of Christianity is no more essential than brands of religions throughout the world, it is a clear indication that Satan's schemes are working in the lives of unbelievers. They have reduced the born- again experience to a religious ritual rather than a relational reconnection to Jehovah; the only true and living God, Father and

Creator of the universe. The sacred writings (Holy Scriptures) establish four exclusive truths that all men must recognize:

- ❖ **There is only one God**; *"There is one God and one mediator between God and men, the Man Christ Jesus."* 1 Timothy 2:5
- ❖ **Jesus is the only way to the Father**; John 14:6; John 10:7, 8; 1 Timothy 2:5.
- ❖ **There is no salvation in any other name**; Acts 4:10, 12.
- ❖ **God has exalted Jesus above all others and requires all men to confess Him as Lord**, Philippians 2:9-11.

These truths carry great weight because they demand urgent response from all people in a way that the religions of the world do not regardless of class, race, gender, color, tongue, or nationality.

Some of the well-known religions of the world are Hindu (2000 B.C), Buddhist (560 B.C.), Islam (610 A.D.), Krishna (965 A.D.), and New Age (1960's).

Each of these religions have extremely different beliefs and focus on one or more gods, either made from material objects or crafted from some form of mystical experience which cannot be validated.

Notice how Jesus Himself imposes the priority of the "born-again" experience on a religious leader that society had identified as a representative of God. This leader came to Him with a set of questions and priorities that did not appear to have anything to do with the requirement that Jesus put forth and emphasized as more important.

John 3:1-17,"*NOW THERE was a certain man among the Pharisees named Nicodemus, a ruler (a leader, an authority) among the Jews, Who came to Jesus at night and said to Him, Rabbi, we know and are certain that You have come from God [as] a Teacher; for no one can do these signs (these wonderworks, these miracles--and produce the proofs) that You do unless God is with him.*

Jesus answered him, I assure you, most solemnly I tell you, that unless a person is born again (anew, from above), he cannot ever see (know, be acquainted with, and experience) the kingdom of God. **Notice how Jesus responded to Nicodemus.** *Nicodemus said to Him, How can a man be born when he is old? Can he enter his mother's womb again and be born?*

Again notice the emphatic urgency of Jesus response. *"Jesus answered, I assure you, most solemnly I tell you, unless a man is born of water and [even] the Spirit, he cannot [ever] enter the kingdom of God. What is born of [from] the flesh is flesh [of the physical is physical]; and what is born of the Spirit is spirit."*

Next, Jesus imposes on Nicodemus a reason to question his own standing with God, even though he is considered a "Teacher of Israel". *"Marvel not [do not be surprised, astonished] at My telling you, You must all be born anew (from above). The wind blows (breathes) where it wills; and though you hear its sound, yet you neither know where it comes from nor where it is going. So it is with everyone who is born of the Spirit.*

Nicodemus answered by asking, how can all this be possible? **Jesus replied, Are you the teacher of Israel, and yet do not know nor understand these things?** *[Are they strange to you? I assure you, most solemnly I tell you, we speak only of what we know [we know absolutely what we are talking about]; we have actually seen what we are testifying to [we were eyewitnesses of it]. And **still you do not receive our testimony [you reject and refuse our evidence--that of Myself and of all those who are born of the Spirit].***

If I have told you of things that happen right here on the earth and yet none of you believes Me, how can you believe [trust Me, adhere to Me, rely on Me] if I tell you of heavenly things?"

And yet no one has ever gone up to heaven, but there is One Who has come down from heaven--the Son of Man [Himself], Who is [dwells, has His home] in heaven.

Finally, He explains the purpose of "the brazen serpent" and its relevance to Himself.

"And just as Moses lifted up the serpent in the desert [on a pole], so must [so it is necessary that] the Son of Man be lifted up [on the cross] In order that everyone who believes in Him [who cleaves to Him, trusts Him, and relies on Him] may not perish, but have eternal life and [actually] live forever! For God

so greatly loved and dearly prized the world that He [even] gave up His only begotten (unique) Son, so that whoever believes in (trusts in, clings to, relies on) Him shall not perish (come to destruction, be lost) but have eternal (everlasting) life."

It does not matter how we rationalize this discourse between Jesus and Nicodemus, the first point clearly stated by Jesus is that unless an individual is "born again" he cannot see [understand, make sense out of, or comprehend] the Kingdom of God [heavenly things].

Clearly from Jesus' point of view, nothing in this life is to be viewed as more important than the inclusion of God and His Kingdom in our individual lives.

Although Nicodemus may have come out of his own motivations to ask Jesus questions that were important to him, Jesus wasted no time explaining the greater priority for Nicodemus and the entire world.

Jesus answered him, *"I assure you, most solemnly I tell you, that unless a person is born again [anew, from above], he cannot ever see [know, be acquainted with, and experience] the kingdom of God."*

Notice how Jesus responded to Nicodemus concerning the necessity of the second birth.

My reason for taking this approach is because I believe that *birth is the beginning of life. However, to be born again is the beginning of a new life* with God through His Son, in His Kingdom. It is to be born from above, to a heavenly life in constant communion with God as a partaker of the divine nature.

This is clearly the first and most important stone to be laid in the foundation of our lives if we are to ever know true success and peace in this life. Our lives must begin with a relationship with God.

Clearly Jesus wasted no time in declaring how important this new birth is before anything God does **can be understood** pertaining to His Kingdom. 1 Corinthians 2:14 explains that the natural man must become a spiritual man before he is capable of receiving and understanding of such things.

"But the natural, non-spiritual man does not accept or welcome or admit into his heart the gifts and teachings and revelations of the Spirit of God, for they are folly (meaningless nonsense) to him; and he is incapable of knowing them [of progressively recognizing, understanding, and becoming better acquainted with them] because they are spiritually discerned and estimated and appreciated.

In that he *"came to Jesus by night,"* Nicodemus seemed to have come to Jesus with his own concerns which perhaps piqued his interest and made him more curious. But, Jesus without hesitation spoke first to what should have been to Nicodemus the most important discussion, *"you must be born again"*. **Here Jesus introduced the experience of "salvation" as mandatory, not just for Nicodemus but all men.**

Chapter 2

The Second Master Key

Self-discovery
Overcoming Social Malpractice

Each day I see so much waste because of misdirected energy, unclear roles, misappropriated assignments, and wrong pieces being forced to conform where they are not designed to fit. Many educational institutions are often consumed with achieving academic excellence and scholastic achievement that they fail to tailor programs to fit individual needs. My conviction is that each student be catered to according their uniqueness, individual gifts, and personal skills, which in my view are their primary needs.

However, it appears that our society is beginning to realize that everyone is not designed to be an educational expert. For years this confusion of focus has distorted the mission of our world causing overcrowding and under achievement by proportions never intended by our Creator.

More of today's educational methods that are systematically determined must result from extensive assessments and evaluations of each child's personal interest during their early and most critical learning years. Then, we must administer the unique education and training model that corresponds to the child's personal needs. If we take this approach, the nation would witness a drastic decline in dropout rates, drug-abuse, crime, violence, teen-pregnancy, single-parent families, and many other hindrances within our communities. I'm not suggesting it would solve all of our social problems, but I am confident it will have a positive impact. Simply put, children would be less stressed and frustrated due to a lack of personal motivation and unforced participation.

Additionally, it would promote increased focus, stimulated interest, and a passionate desire in learning institutions. I say this because I almost drowned in the system under the radar due to a variety of undetected problems during my elementary and middle school years. Even though, I tried very hard initially, it felt like doors were closing rapidly from every side. I shut myself in and through misdirected pride, I kept others out. Even those in positions to help were not allowed to assist me.

I remember vividly the frustrations I kept vaulted inside that swiftly became my fear of not being able to cope. I was not able to understand academics like my siblings, relatives, or classmates. Afraid of letting my parents down, I was intimidated by the scholastic achievements of my elder sister and embarrassed by the accelerated accomplishments of my younger brother. This, for me, was a real trap.

I remember when relatives and neighborhood families would come together during report card time to proudly share the grades of their children. I never looked forward to those times. For a while I seemed only able to consistently earn an "A" in conduct. My parents were hard working and very caring; always busy creating opportunities for us. My siblings were smart and my family and friends were very caring. Yet, I perceived this network of support as pressure to do better. But it seemed that the harder I tried, the more difficult it became to comprehend the classroom lessons.

One day, I remember sitting at the dining table approximately forty-five minutes to an hour trying to solve one math problem so I could play basketball. Back then, we were not allowed to do anything after school until our homework and house chores were completed. My younger brother walked in, looked over my shoulder, and pointed his finger at the page and said, "This is simple bro. Change this, move that over, erase the way you started off, and that's it. Now, let's go play ball, man, you're holding us up!"

I was embarrassed and insulted by my brother's forwardness to solve my problem without my consent. So, after he walked out the room, I changed this, moved that over, and erased the way I started off, finished my remaining homework and went outside to play basketball. This made me very uncomfortable, because I viewed myself as a slow learner. He, on the other hand, was very competitive and unpredictable which I knew he would bring up later which would cause me to feel even more intellectually inferior. But I did it anyway.

The next day in school I turned in my assignment, the teacher graded it, the answer was correct. I was nervously excited because I could sense something else brewing. Well, just as I feared, Mrs. Pilot called out my name, "Finace!" I immediately went into a daze. "Finace Bush," I sat numb as she asked, "Would you please go to the board and show us how you got your answer?"

I paused, getting up slowly while grasping my paper. "Without your paper" she said. There I was, partially leaning on my desk, looking despondent, and feeling exasperated in front of the entire class. I think I would have fainted had she not said, "That's ok Finace, we won't have time enough to finish before the bell rings." Oh my! What a temporary relief. Little did I know that things were about to change for me. God was doing something I could not have discerned in the slightest.

As I prepared to exit the class, my teacher, Mrs. Pilot, asked me to stay behind for a few minutes. Staring me in the center of my eyes, she asked, "Finace, did you do this or did someone else do it for you?" I replied, "Yes I did it but my sister helped me." Everyone at school knew my sister because she was a high achiever and very athletic. Piercing my heart with a blinkless stare, Mrs. Pilot said, "You don't have to be ashamed son, I've noticed how hard you work and I want you to keep working hard, it'll come."

Mrs. Pilot could see through my nervousness that something was wrong, but instead of embarrassing me she asked if I would like to meet with her during breaks or remain after class a few minutes a day to review assignments until I understood the basics. In retrospect, it became increasingly clear to me that receiving help from Mrs. Pilot was so significant and created a turning point in my life academically and spiritually. What began as a problem, turned out to be a great privilege. My light affliction, which was but for a moment, was working for me and if these sequence of events had not occurred I may not have gotten beyond my hidden fear that was rooted in deceitful pride.

It's interesting that the teacher named *Mrs. Pilot* was the one who demonstrated the kind of interest that encouraged me to "stay with it until I got the basics." And my younger brother, smarter than me academically, who advised me to "change that, move this, and erase that" were both used as catalyst to push me in the direction of my destiny.

I have used these two instructive disciplines many times in my life over the years, which came from two divinely appointed destiny travelers.

Reminiscent of my experience, I compared it with biblical truths that were revealed through prayer and meditation. In this, I discovered that God plants new beginnings through strange encounters.

God Births New Beginnings from Strange Encounters

"Life is a maze for those who have no personal identity." In the sixteenth chapter and nineteenth verse of the Gospel of Matthew, Jesus said, *"I will give you the keys of the kingdom of heaven;"* (AMP). This phrase signified a kind of special power and divine right to Peter. Key's are important and significant symbols in life. Often, the person who has no key is not able to enter doors of opportunities.

In this case, the privilege of the keys meant that Peter would be a steward of the household of God; opening the door for men to enter into the Kingdom. Peter's response redefined his entire existence, unveiled his destiny, and set the stage for a life of purpose and fulfillment.

Self-discovery is the Key to Personal Fulfillment

The critical key necessary for the consistent enjoyment of a fulfilled life is *self-discovery*. Many people have no idea who they are or what their purpose is, nor do they fully comprehend how to obtain these insights. I think the words of an anonymous patriarch says it best; "Usually a man does what he can until his destiny is revealed."

Jesus said to Peter: *"Peter, your name means a rock, and **your destiny** is to be a rock. You are the first man among the brethren to recognize me for what I am, and therefore you are the first stone in the edifice of the fellowship of those who are mine. In the days to come, **you must be the steward who unlocks the doors** of the kingdom that all men may enter."* (Matthew 16:18, 19)

How We Function Best

Peter made a discovery; however, along with his discovery he was given a great privilege and responsibility. It is a discovery that everyone must make for themselves and when this discovery is made, similar privileges and responsibilities are placed upon him. It is my conviction that we are all more effective when we function according to the uniqueness of our design instead of under the pressures we place on ourselves when attempting that which we are incapable of and lack the qualifications to perform.

Much like automobiles or high-tech devices, the potential of all humans can be greatly exploited or on the other hand appreciated if used according to the Creator's design and purpose.

Individuals who have not discovered their identity or purpose, in most cases, cannot discern where they fit, where they want to go in life, how to discern appropriate friendships and associations, the type of career paths that best satisfies their existence, or other critical issues that determine the quality of life.

Without knowing who we are, why we were created, or where we fit, it is very difficult to fulfill our God given purpose. Without purpose, we feel insignificant and unnecessary and ultimately make us vulnerable, frustrated, socially and morally bankrupt, easily offended, and self-destructive. So, I ask you, are you functioning according to the uniqueness of your design?

Our Best Example

A close observation of Jesus' life illustrates the power and privilege of self-discovery:

> "Now it happened as they journeyed on the road, that someone said to Him, "Lord, I will follow you wherever you go." And Jesus said to him, "Foxes have holes and birds of the air have nests, but the Son of Man has nowhere to lay His head." Then He said to another, "Follow Me." But he said, "Lord, let me first go and bury my father." Jesus said to him, "Let the dead bury their own dead, but **you go and preach** the kingdom of God." And another also said, "Lord, I will follow You, but let me first go and bid them farewell who are at my house." But Jesus said to him, "**No one**, having put his hand to the plow, and **looking back, is fit** for the kingdom of God" (Luke 9:57-62, NKJV).

These things Jesus said to establish: *the urgency of kingdom business* and to ensure that *we maximize our potential by prioritizing our initiatives to correspond with our personal mission.* These passages also reflect the importance of time management which essentially is personal management. How you use your time today is a barometer for tomorrow's prosperity.

Jesus did not allow relationship crisis or conditions of urgency to alter his course. It was certainly God's will that determined His **direction**, His **timing**, and definitely His **priorities**. Notice that He kept his priorities on point in the story of Lazarus:

> "Now **a certain man** was sick, Lazarus of Bethany, the town of Mary and her sister Martha. **It was that Mary who anointed** the Lord with fragrant oil **and wiped His feet** with her hair, whose brother Lazarus was sick. Therefore **the sisters sent to Him**, saying, "Lord, behold, he whom you love is sick." When Jesus heard that, He said, "This sickness is not unto death, but for the glory of God, that the Son of God might be glorified through it." Now **Jesus loved** Martha and her sister and Lazarus. So, **when He heard** that he was sick, **He stayed two more days in the place where He was.**

[Today, these circumstances, in many cases, would have required an urgent response and Jesus' seemingly insensitive lack of response would have been harshly judged.]

Then after this He said to the disciples, "Let us go to Judea again." The disciples said to Him, "Rabbi, lately the Jews sought to stone You, and are You going there again?" Jesus answered, "Are there not twelve hours in the day? If anyone walks in the day, he does not stumble, because he sees the light of this world. But if one walks in the night, he stumbles because the light is not in him." These things He said, and after that He said to them, "Our friend Lazarus sleeps, but I go that I may wake him up." Then His disciples said, "Lord, if he sleeps he will get well." However, Jesus spoke of his death, but they thought that He was speaking about taking rest in sleep. Then Jesus said to them plainly, "Lazarus is dead. And I am glad for your sakes that I was not there, that you may believe. Nevertheless let us go to him.

Then Thomas, who is called the Twin, said to his fellow disciples, "Let us also go, that we may die with Him." So **when Jesus came, He found that he had already been in the tomb four days.** *Now Bethany was near Jerusalem, about two miles away. And many of the Jews had joined the women around Martha and Mary, to comfort them concerning their brother.*

Now Martha, as soon as she heard that Jesus was coming, went and met Him, but Mary was sitting in the house. Now **Martha** *said to Jesus, "Lord,* **if You had been here,** *my brother would not have died. But even now I know that whatever You ask of God, God will give You." Jesus said to her, "Your brother will rise again. ..."*

... Then, when Mary came where Jesus was, and saw Him, she fell down at His feet, saying to Him, "Lord, **if you had been here,** *my brother would not have died"* (John 11:1-32, NKJV).

Clearly, Jesus fully understood His mission. Understanding His mission allowed Him to direct His focus on daily priorities with laser-beam intensity. He was committed to accomplishing daily task without personal distractions or the demands of others near and dear to Him. His preparation and planning enabled Him to establish, what I refer to as, structured priorities which conditioned Him to *avoid confusion of responsibility and ownership of Himself.* He knew who He was and why He was sent, therefore, *He stayed on His course.*

You too must begin to experience a daily lifestyle that maximizes your personal uniqueness and ability. You must do so without infringing on the personal responsibility and assignments of others. Remember, confusion of our responsibility and ownership is due to a lack of *structured priorities.* This is a result of not knowing who you are.

Failed Attempts
Striving Without Priorities

As overseer and mentor it is my most frequent observation that too often Believers take for granted the importance of managing their priorities and creating solid business habits which would allow them to prove to themselves that God really does bless them when they obey His Word.

For many years, I experienced blessings but had no tracking systems to neither confirm nor measure God's involvement. I was like so many religious people who wonder why God does not seem to be concerned about their struggles, so they take life issues in their own hands and live as if their assessments are accurate. Proverbs 16:25 implies that what seems right are actually ways of death. In other words, each attempt makes their situation worst because good assumptions are not confirmed like truth.

Throughout this book I talk candidly about the life I experienced without managing

my priorities effectively and the upgraded quality of life I now experience daily as a result of putting first things first. The Holy Spirit once said to me that "As long as you assume what's right, you will continue to live in error and forfeit God's best."

Here's the point you cannot miss; I am not implying that I was not reading , praying, studying, meditating, confessing, giving, doing good and living right as we sometimes say." The problem I had, like many others, is that although I was consistently carrying out my daily rituals and routines I was not working the Word of God effectively in my life that would have allowed it to shape my views and change my approach in the way I managed my affairs.

Somehow I assumed that my ways were sufficient to guide and defend my life without even considering that God was only a ritual and religious practice I had included much like entertainment and sports. Once I got tired of reading and hearing what the Word said about my situations and looking at the differences in what it implied against my frustrated and bankrupt natural and spiritual life, I finally got it.

I knew I had a relationship with God because I was knowingly converted at age twelve, but things just weren't adding up. How could God possibly prove Himself to me when I was squandering everything He'd blessed me with?

After thirty years of attempting to be superman, spiderman, ghost-buster, lifesaver, the equalizer, and many other super-friends, I learned that life offers each of us opportunities. From these opportunities we either succeed or fail at them. How we decide to pursue them, and the standards and methods we apply to set our priorities determine the overall effectiveness of our impact on society. It also determines the daily level of joy and comfort we experience.

Therefore, our *structured priorities* should emanate based on our destiny and not as a temporary patch for the moment. Anyone who bases his or her response to life on crisis or favor that arises from a 'moment' may never know lasting success or the peaceful habitation that the Creator intended us to experience.

Uniqueness Requires Attention

We are all unique individuals. Some are exceptionally

talented athletically and born with natural adroitness and agility that exceeds training. Some have perceptional gifts and skilled in multiple ways. Yet, there are some who possess skills and abilities but are searching to find their niche that makes them unique. They might search for the thing that not only makes them different, but will galvanize their passion with purpose and set them on a path to a peaceful and successful life.

Our development of that uniqueness ensures that we have the ability to contribute our uniqueness to the society designed by our awesome Creator. When we observe how a world map is structured to define boundaries for continents, countries, states, and cities, we see communities with physical property lines that distinguish ownership and preserve personal interest.

As a structured society, we must set spiritual, mental, emotional, and physical boundaries to define what is and is not our personal responsibility. Although you and I possess the skills necessary to perform certain tasks, without structured boundaries we lack the ability to adequately manage our time, money, relationships, and occupations.

The inability to structure our lives to maximize our potential and satisfy the demands of our existence is a serious problem. Failure to set appropriate boundaries at appropriate times with appropriate people is self–destructive behavior. Dedicated Believers are often confused about when it is 'biblically appropriate' to set limits or draw boundary lines when extending their 'undeveloped selves.'

An Experiment That Paid Dividends

During the first three months of carefully observing my activities, I began structuring my daily functions. These are a few of the questions I was confronted with in the process:

1. Where do I begin?
2. What things should I consider first?

3. Is it possible to set limits and still be viewed as a loving person?
4. What if my family and close friends don't understand?
5. How will I respond to those who want my time, energy, or money when it is neither convenient nor appropriate for me?
6. Why do I feel guilty or afraid when considering potential conflicts with those who frequently interact with me?
7. How should structure apply to the roles within my marriage and parenting, daily devotion, exercise, work, ministry, diet, and rest so that I am effective?
8. Should I feel my need for "structure" is a selfish endeavor?

I was able to rediscover my true life and purpose through clear biblical references that addressed these questions specifically and silenced this internal ambivalence I contended with daily. It also delivered me from the turmoil and mediocrity that had dominated my life for so long. Sometimes ambivalent feelings that linger result from a lack of knowledge or uncertainty about individual rights and positions to take during certain exchanges with others close to you.

For example, during my young adult years I earned so much money through multiple streams of income that sometimes I would neglect my priorities to help my friends and associates who always seemed to struggle. At one time, I became a surety for three special friends, two preachers, and one relative. I had yet to learn that surety or co-signing for individuals was not wise according to the Scripture, especially for friends who did not have a proven record of faithfulness nor assets with enough value for collateral.

Proverbs 6:1 and 17:18 revealed to me that I was violating myself and my primary responsibilities for lacking wisdom of the Scriptures, assuming that God would have done the same thing. Like Jesus said in Matthew 22;29, *"You're off base on two counts: You don't know your Bibles, and you don't know how God works."(The Message)*

Only after the two preachers relocated miles away, ruined my credit, and left me with the responsibility of paying their debt, the Holy Spirit revealed what I was ready to learn. My teacher would often say to me, "Finace, when the student in you shows up, the teacher will emerge." At that time, life can use anything necessary to teach you.

This is a great reason to learn the principle of association to avoid unnecessary demands that others may impose on you through their access. I will discuss this principle in greater detail in the ingredients of "time, money and relationships."

This simplified revelation will empower you to regain ownership and responsibility of your "true self" through Kingdom principles empowered by the Holy Spirit. Self-discovery through Christ is an experience everyone should desire. It will rescue you from clinical psychological symptoms such as depression, anxiety disorders, eating disorders, addictions, impulsive disorders, guilt, problems in marriage and relationships with family and friends, which are deeply rooted in *"you"* due to a lack of understanding and need for a *structured lifestyle that corresponds with your expectations.* This revelation will enable you to understand proper ways to employ and apply faith to secure the manifestation of God's promises in your life.

My goal is to enable every Believer to realize that God has equipped each of us uniquely for success through the examples and patterns demonstrated by Christ and many others mentioned in His word. Before you complete this book it is my hope that you will agree with me that the only problem with structure is that you have lived too long without it!

The principle disciplines of structure are like ingredients designed to enhance you wholesomely through the ability to master your-self. Any attempt to master others is simply a waste of time.

Dr. Stephen R. Covey so eloquently stated, "Often in our relationships we want to control other people. At the same time, we resist their attempts to control us, scarcely remembering that if we resist control, they no doubt resist it as well. The fact is, neither we, nor they can be controlled by anyone else. We are each responsible for our own control."

Genesis 1:26 says, "And God said, "*Let us make man in our image, after our likeness: and let them have dominion over the fish of the sea, and over the fowl of the air, and over the cattle, and over all the earth, and over every creeping thing that creepeth upon the earth.*"

Notice, God never said dominate, master, or lord over man. However, He did take precious time to identify the specific things of which mankind ("*them*") is to share dominion. God must have been very serious about the specificity of this assignment because immediately after He created man, in verse twenty-seven, He reiterated His divine will for [them] man, in verse twenty-eight:

Notice, "*And God blessed them, and said to them, Be fruitful, and multiply, and replenish the earth, and subdue it: and have dominion over the fish of the sea, and over the fowl of the air, and over every living thing that moveth upon the earth.*"

Chapter 3

The Third Master Key

The Power of the Pattern

Now, if you followed closely through each of the points presented you probably realize that a **pattern** has been established for Kingdom citizens who are *"willing and obedient"* that guarantees **success**. Once you accept Jesus Christ as your Savior you are well on your way.

Scriptures clarify that God intended for each new Kingdom citizen to develop spiritually through discipleship designed to overcome issue after issue until our "being" and "doing" experience change. This is designed for each new convert to adopt the Kingdom's way as a new lifestyle.

The Bible carefully illustrates how Jesus (the ultimate example) who was faithful in prayer, Bible study, and discipline training, entered into His ministry filled with the Spirit, well prepared and qualified at the age of thirty.

Enlightened to His purpose, Jesus began fulfilling His mission. He also had a firm understanding of His Father's *will* through Scripture. He called twelve others whom He mentored (trained and discipled) according to Kingdom principles. He supervised and navigated their development, while He accomplished His mission.

All established spiritual guides and instructors (pastors/teachers/mentors) should assist in the development of students through teaching and training them to follow the example of Christ. The point here is that success should be second nature for Christians. Jesus left us a pattern that should be to convey through well-planned training sessions.

*"For I have given you an example, **that ye should do** as I have done to you"* (John 13:15, KJV).

*"Let this **mind** be in you, which was also in Christ Jesus: Who, being in the form of God, thought it not robbery to be equal with God:"* (Philippians 2:5, KJV).

"For even hereunto were ye called: because Christ also suffered for us, leaving us an example, that ye should follow his steps:" (1 Peter 2:21, KJV).

The Bible clearly teaches that when you walk according to the pattern that Christ has designed and left. This pattern dictates success in those specific areas. Not temporary success, but continued success throughout your life as you stay within this pattern.

What has happened to Christendom!

Today, too many clergy and religious superiors are sporting and pleasing themselves by satisfying their personal, racial, and social agendas. Some use carnal reasoning and religious services that cater to their selfish desires and non-scriptural practices. This leaves the door open for demonic forces to gain ground by using schemes and devices that accelerate widespread satanic philosophies which can cripple the impact of the Word of God. Jesus addressed the religious leaders of His day for establishing similar services.

*"Then came to Jesus scribes and Pharisees, which were of Jerusalem, saying, Why do thy disciples transgress the tradition of the elders? for they wash not their hands when they eat bread. But he answered and said unto them, Why do **ye** also transgress the commandment of God by your tradition? For God commanded, saying, Honor thy father and mother: and, He that curseth father or mother, let him die the death. But ye say, Whosoever shall say to his father or his mother, It is a gift, by whatsoever thou mightest be profited by me; And honour not his father or his mother, he shall be free. Thus have **ye** made the commandment of God of none effect by your tradition."* (Mathew 15:1-6)

Today, throughout the world in places of worship, we are faced with perplexities and diversities of troubles on every side resulting from the neglect and ignorance of essential principles. It is time for Kingdom Believers to begin aligning their operations and daily functions with Kingdom righteousness that pertains to godliness and fully corresponds with His will for us.

In order for any of us to experience effective Christianity, it must be understood that we must be trained as disciples to demonstrate God's way. It is a model way of doing and being that sets parameters for Believers' attitudes and practices to direct their destiny. In other words, it is to teach, train, and develop the spiritual fruit of discipline within each Believer. It is why Paul says, *"Follow me as I follow Christ."* Many times it's easier to communicate God's intentions by examples and illustrations, rather than oral and written lessons.

Those who fail to operate according to God's way because of traditions not inspired by God simply *"transgress the commandments of God"* by the man-made tradition, thus *"making the commandment of God of no effect."* These persons, according to Paul, have a zeal *for God, but not according to knowledge.*

Notice, they have a "zeal" (an intense enthusiasm and a passion; they are fanatics), *but, not according to what is proper and acceptable to God.* Here again, their methods, traditions, systems, practices, or convictions were not justified or authorized, therefore, could not be confirmed according to correct and vital knowledge.

"... For they being ignorant of God's righteousness, and seeking to establish their own righteousness, have not submitted to the righteousness of God." (Romans 10:2-3, NKJV). This is the result of non-effective, shallow Christianity.

Paul cautions the Colossians; *Beware lest any man spoil you through philosophy and vain deceit, after the tradition of men, after the rudiments of the world, and not after Christ.* (Colossians 2.8)

The Amplified version clarifies; *See to it that no one carries you off as spoil or make you yourselves captive by his so-called philosophy and intellectualism and vain deceit (idle fancies and plain nonsense), following **human tradition** (men's ideas of **the material rather than the spiritual world),** just crude notions following the rudimentary and elemental teachings of the universe and disregarding [the teachings of] Christ (the Messiah).*

As Believers we must make sure that what we extract from God's Word reflects Christ and the standards, goals, and objectives He communicated in His teachings, lest we lose the essence of the Kingdom's way. *"Search the scriptures; for in them ye think ye have eternal life: and they are they which testify of me"* (John 5.39).

Success Simplified
The Power of the Pattern

In the Gospel of John chapter 13 verses 15-17, Jesus states that: "For I have given you this as an example, so that you should do [in your turn] what I have done to you. I assure you, most solemnly I tell you, a servant is not greater than his master, and no one who is sent is superior to the one who sent him. If you know these things, blessed and happy and to be envied are you if you practice them [if you act accordingly and really do them]" (AMP).

A closer examination of these passages allows us to see the simplicity of Godly success. Notice in verse 15, Jesus first emphasizes the importance of His example. The Webster Dictionary defines "example" as something selected to show the nature or character of the rest; a person or thing to be imitated modeled or patterned (Dictionary.com, LLC s.d.).

Clearly, we may understand from this definition that Jesus selected opportunities and events to show His disciples (followers) the importance of duplicating and imitating His pattern (example). In fact, verse 14 states that He obligated His disciples to imitate Him.

I must admit, this is where my life began to turn around in a way that allowed God to extend His grace into my life in a loving way. The Scriptures declare *examples* to be God's way of transferring Kingdom inheritance to the body of Christ.

Notice what Apostle Paul wrote to the Hebrew converts;

"In order that you may not grow disinterested and become [spiritual] sluggards, but imitators, behaving as do those who through faith (by their leaning of the entire personality on God in Christ in absolute trust and confidence in His power, wisdom, and goodness) and by practice of patient endurance and waiting are [now] inheriting the promises" (Hebrews 6:12, AMP).

Predestined and Guaranteed Success

Following a pattern practically guarantees, at a minimum, consistent results in most cases. So, if the pattern is positive the results are going to be positive, but if the pattern is negative the results are going to be negative. The success of every Believer has already been determined when we structure or lives to follow the biblical examples and patterns that Christ has patterned for us and sealed with His blood.

When a seamstress is contracted to make fifty choir robes, the initial design and structure of the first pattern may be difficult. But, after the first robe is completed, the other forty-nine becomes relatively easy and less time consuming due to the success of the first. This is also true in the case of blueprints and road maps. A blueprint may be difficult to draft, but upon completion, a builder only needs to be committed to following the details in order to construct a successful structure.

Most of us take great ease in getting into our automobiles and successfully traveling to and from our destinations. But how often are we mindful of the time, energy, and the number of lives that were sacrificed for our ease? Following an already established map (or pattern) is actually an accelerated guarantee to a successful journey.

This was the key to the success of the old patriarchs who succeeded Abraham; from Isaac to Joseph. The same concept or principle guaranteed Joshua's success. Joshua walked according to the predetermined laws that God had already established by his mentor, Moses.

The Key to Joshua's Ministry

An Old Testament Example

The success of Joshua's ministry was inevitable because of the blueprint established by Moses. God instructed Moses to take Joshua and transfer his spirit upon him. The Bible says that Joshua received the same spirit that was upon Moses (Numbers 27:15-23). Afterwards, when God visited Joshua, he immediately reminded him to do what Moses his mentor said, in order to succeed. This is found in **Joshua 1:1-8:**

*"Now after the death of Moses the servant of the LORD it came to pass, that the LORD spake unto Joshua the son of Nun, Moses' minister, saying, Moses my servant is dead; now therefore arise, go over the Jordan, thou, and all this people, unto the land which I do give to them, even to the children of Israel. Every place that the sole of your foot shall tread upon, that have I given unto you, as I said unto Moses. From the wilderness and this Lebanon even unto the great river, the river Euphrates, all the land of the Hittites, and unto the great sea toward the going down of the sun, shall be your coast. There shall not any man be able to stand before thee all the days of thy life: as I was with Moses, so I will be with thee: I will not fail thee, nor forsake thee. Be strong and of a good courage: for unto this people shalt thou divide for an inheritance the land, which I sware unto their fathers to give them. Only be thou strong and very courageous, that thou mayest observe to do according to all the law, which Moses my servant commanded thee: turn not from it to the right hand or to the left, that thou mayest prosper withersoever thou goest. This book of the **law shall not depart** out of thy mouth; but **thou shalt meditate** therein day and night, that thou mayest **observe to do** according to all that is written therein: for then thou shalt **make thy way prosperous**, and then thou shalt have good success.*

Realize that true success has a blue print to follow. The route to it has already been established. There are many non-believers, discovering the way to secular success every day. Often, they use biblical information without a relationship with God and without a license to practice what's in the Book, while many Believers remain slothful and full of excuses. For that reason we need to look at 1 Corinthians chapter nine as one of the foundational scriptures to use in applying "structure." It is here that the Apostle Paul addresses the discipline it takes when striving for the mastery.

Striving for a Mastery

In 1 Corinthians 9:25, Paul states: "*And every man that strives for mastery is **temperate** in all things....*" Paul asserts that we must commit ourselves to run in the race. But, we must "stop beating at the air." Each of us are uniquely fashioned with a distinct purpose and a chief aim in life. Discovering our purpose should motivate us to set clear goals. Those goals should be clarified and refined through the Word of God. Here Paul cautions Believers not to *beat at the* air, or in other words, waste time with things outside our central purpose; "*I don't fight an uncertain fight anymore,*" he says. To paraphrase what Paul is saying; I am not the feet attempting to perform as a hand. I am not a heart, acting like a liver. I study my purpose carefully based on how God designed me and the positions I hold. Then, by focusing my attention on who I am, I can then understand what I have to contribute.

Finally, with these things in perspective I *keep my body under* subjection to predetermined, corresponding disciplines lest I fail to accomplish that which is set before me. Life is filled with many issues. Even so, the heart too has many issues to address. As the hard drive of a computer waits for instructions to be dictated to determine the function it will perform. So is the heart of man waiting for the correct instructions to be dictated from the Word of God to direct the proper ways to effectively function.

When wisdom suggests that we "guard our hearts with all diligence," the hint is to provoke us to be structured in every area pertaining to our personhood. Note that to further affirm this point, Wisdom strengthens her assertion by finishing this thought with "*for out of it are the issues of life!*"

This must be done in every personal and relational aspect of our manifest of life. We must begin with the prioritizing of our *three-part* or *triune* being. Then, properly assigning our time, we are to establish a mission for our money (resources) and clarify a vision for our family, develop the right attitude for work or occupation, and define our relationships to avoid unnecessary distractions and hindrances (using each of the principle ingredients of structure). This is what the Apostle Paul made clear in his first letter to the Believers at Corinth.

"*Every Man that Striveth for the Mastery must be Temperate in all Things.*" Other scriptures that encourages Believers to follow the pattern:

❖ **1 Peter 2.21: Peter reiterated the importance and power of the pattern.**

For to this you were called [it is inseparable from your vocation]. *Because Christ also suffered for you, leaving you* [it is personal] **an example,** *that* **you should follow** *on in His footsteps.* (*NKJV*)

For to this you were called, because Christ also suffered for us, leaving us **an example,** that we should **follow His steps** (*NKJV*). **The** Apostle Paul advises the church in several of his Epistles to follow the pattern that was established through Christ:

❖ **Hebrews 12:1-3 outlines a five-step concept** (discussed in greater detail in the chapter, "*Lay Aside the Weight.*")

Therefore we also, since we are surrounded by so great a cloud of witnesses, let us lay aside every weight, and the sin which so easily ensnares us, and let us run with endurance the race that is set before us. Looking unto Jesus, the author and finisher of our faith, who for the joy that was set before Him endured the cross, despising the shame, and has sat down at the right hand *of the throne of God. For **consider Him** who endured such hostility from sinners against Himself, lest you become weary and discouraged in your souls. (NKJV)*

❖ Philippians 2:5-8 outlines examples of Christ's humility in seven steps.

Let this mind be in you which was also in Christ Jesus, who, being in the form of God, did not consider it robbery to be equal with God, but made Himself of no reputation, taking the form of a bondservant, and coming in the likeness of men. And being found in appearance as a man, He humbled Himself and became obedient to the point of death, even the death of the cross.

❖ Philippians 3:12-14 provides a three step description necessary to obtain the goal that lies ahead.

Not that I have already attained, or am already perfected: but I press on, that I may lay hold of that for which Christ Jesus has also laid hold of me.

Brethren, I do not count myself to have apprehended; but one thing I do, forgetting those things which are behind and reaching forward to those things which are ahead, I press toward the goal for the prize of the upward call of God in Christ Jesus.

❖ Philippians 4.8-9, defining the things necessary to set one's mind to be productive.

Finally, brethren, whatever things are true, whatever things are noble, whatever things are just, whatever things are pure, whatever things are lovely, whatever things are of good report, if there is any virtue and if there is anything praiseworthy - meditate on these things. The things which you learned and received and heard and saw in me, these do, and the God of peace will be with you.

❖ Ephesians 6:11-17 :The armor needed to conquer satanic and contrary forces.

Put on the whole armor of God, that you may be able to stand against the wiles of the devil. For we do not wrestle against flesh and blood, but against principalities, against powers, against the rulers of the darkness of this age, against spiritual hosts of wickedness in the heavenly places. Therefore take up the whole armor of God, that you may be able to withstand in the evil day, and having done all, to stand. Stand therefore, having girded you waist with truth, having put on the breastplate of righteousness, and having shod your feet with the preparation of the gospel of peace; above all, taking the shield of faith with which you will be able to quench all the fiery darts of the wicked one. And take the helmet of salvation, and the sword of the Spirit, which is the word of God;

❖ Galatians 6.1-2: Paul outlines the application needed to restore fallen brethren.

Brethren, if a man is overtaken in any trespass, you who are spiritual restore such a one in a spirit of gentleness, considering yourself lest you also be tempted. Bear one another's burdens, and so fulfill the law of Christ.

There are many other patterns listed throughout the Scripture, which if applied, will generate significant Godly success!

Chapter 4

The Curse of Mediocrity

"A subtle time-induced stronghold is developed through a disoriented state of mind; distorted by satanic deception to rob God's people of their inheritance." - **Finace Bush Jr.**

If we are to live principle driven lives that will bring forth a fruitful Kingdom lifestyle, we must recognize what mediocrity is. *Mediocrity* is the acceptance of ineffectiveness of a method or systematic operation. In many cases, the processes consist of an unwillingness to abandon old practices or methods that no longer work.

It is much like the contemporary definition of **"insanity"** (doing the same thing, the same way, but expecting different results). It can become a hurdle in the life of every Believer who has not adopted God's Kingdom lifestyle. I call it the lifestyle of faith. If we accept anything as a way of life, as a system of belief and as a means of communicating or operating in this earth system (*other than what God says is an acceptable standard for life*); that is to operate in mediocrity. "Whatsoever is not of faith is sin." (Romans 14:23)

To expound further, **mediocrity** is neither implies good or bad according to Webster's Dictionary. In other words, to operate in mediocrity means to operate in the middle. The one place that God despises in the Kingdom is life in the middle.

In fact, in Revelation 3:15, 16, God says, *"I know your [record of] works and what you are doing; you are neither cold nor hot. Would **that you were cold or hot!** So, because you are lukewarm and neither cold nor hot, I will spew you out of My mouth!"* (AMP)

Sometimes this Scripture is taken out of context. God never said that you can't be cold, nor did He promote hot above cold. He said I'd rather you be either hot or cold. Listen, every church will not be hot, nor will every church be cold. If you study the passage in context you will see that the region the text is extracted from had two climates in it. One climate was very cold; the other climate was very hot.

Jesus said neither one of those climates bothered God, He likes both. There is a time when heat is the very thing I need, there is also a time when cold is the appropriate climate. But what He doesn't like is the in-between. It makes God sick. In my personal opinion, lukewarm climates or in-between weather conditions generate more sicknesses and viruses than any other seasonal conditions each year.

Mediocre People are not Successful

Mediocrity is also defined as ordinary; to be average. It's amazing how many Believers are satisfied with being average. They commonly feel as though they are like everybody else. This is a disoriented mind-set. This type of closed-mind keeps a person estranged and alienated from the life God has predestined for them.

The reality of salvation means that there is an anointing on life that makes everyone better than before. No longer are we common persons as spouses, parents, pastors, sons, brothers, friends, on the job, during leisure, recreational activities, nor in any other necessary functional lifestyle situation where performance is an issue.

You must realize that as a child of God, you are a new class of people! *"Transformed from the kingdom of darkness into the kingdom of light. A royal priesthood, a peculiar nation, and a chosen generation of people."*

Mediocrity means ordinary; average; "NOT GOOD ENOUGH" (Dictionary.com).

It means that you don't have the kind of structure that enables you to rise or succeed. The ability, through your own philosophy, to rise above ordinary or common crisis in life is not there. **You tell**

yourself you're not good enough.

It also means the acceptance of inferiority; it's the absence of ability to compete with others because you don't realize you possess what it takes. You can't imagine yourself living in above average conditions. You don't have enough wind beneath your wings to fly. It says that you are just not cut out for it. **Mediocrity is a curse!**

In his Epistle to the Ephesians, Paul encourages Believers to make sure they have the right mindset to avoid alienation or being cut off from the life of God because of ignorance.

This I say therefore, and testify in the Lord, that ye henceforth walk not at other Gentiles walk **in the vanity of their mind***, having their understanding darkened, being* **alienated** *from the life of God* **through** *the* **ignorance** *that is* **in them, because of the blindness** *of their* **heart***.*

Who being past feeling have given themselves over unto lasciviousness, to work all uncleanness with greediness. But **have not so learned Christ***; If so be that ye have heard him, and have been taught by him, as the truth is in Jesus: That ye put off concerning the former conversation the old man, which is corrupt according to the deceitful lusts; And* **be renewed in the spirit of your mind***,* Ephesians. 4:17-23 (KJV)

The most significant reason that mediocrity must not be practiced from the Believers is because it is a subtle time induced stronghold developed in a disoriented state of mind, distorted by satanic deception, to rob God's people of their inheritance.

Mediocrity is the dysfunctional system that keeps Kingdom citizens bound to poverty stricken, menial, and non-progressive conditions. Their lack of knowledge usually results in disenfranchised citizenship. It is the only futile mind-set that suggests that we can never work in a better job, culture, or climate because of presumed limitations. That we cannot move up in life. That we should never dream of living in better houses or owning more than one at a time.

It also suggests that we cannot own luxurious and sporty cars while living in extravagant homes, while striving to please God. That we certainly cannot clothe ourselves in high-fashion apparel and own these things at the same time. Remember, the Bible emphatically states that *"the earth is the Lord's!"*

Other Diabolical Satanic Effects of Mediocrity

Mediocrity also prevents talented people from even dreaming of starting their own companies or developing concepts and ideas that may be worth millions. It prevents God-inspired insights that could acquire freedom and create better opportunities for families, friends, and others throughout communities.

The good news is, you don't have to accept that the job you have is where you must stay for the next forty years because it's what your parents did. You do not have to accept living in the same starter home for the rest of your life just because your immediate family and neighborhood peers expect you to. Neither do you have to succumb to the limits that some misguided religious and secular persons will try to impose on you.

God's promises yield provision for those who work according to his plan. "He came that you might have life and that more abundantly." The truth is, God's desire is to see you live life as He lives it. Remember, you are His child and as with earthly Fathers, they desire for their children to live a qualitative and purposeful life.

God's Ultimate Desire
To Give You the Good Life!

In John 10.10, Jesus made a very insightful declaration. *"I have come that you may have life and that you may have it more abundantly."* Note, the word He used for "life" in the original Greek is "Zoë," denoting life as a principle, life as God has it; that which the Father has in Himself and that which He gave to His son to have in Himself.

In other words, God's purpose for sending His Son was to give us "Life" as He lives it through a system called Kingdom righteousness. This is the primary reason Jesus encouraged all new converts to first seek the Kingdom of God and His righteousness. It is through the Kingdom of God's system that we rediscover the God life which is actually the proper way to live.

To further support this claim, notice John 5.26 of the Amplified: *"For even as the Father has life in Himself and is self-existent, so He has given to the Son to have life in Himself and be self-existent."*

*"This I say therefore, and testify in the Lord, that ye henceforth walk not as other Gentiles walk, in the vanity of their mind, Having the understanding darkened, being **alienated from the life of God through the ignorance** that is in them, because of **the blindness of their heart."*** (Ephesians 4.17, 18).

The Holy Spirit Also Cries out Through the Apostle

Romans 12:1, 2

*"I beseech you therefore, brethren, by the mercies of God that you present your bodies a living sacrifice, holy, acceptable unto God, which is your reasonable service. And be not conformed to this world: but be ye transformed **by the renewing of your mind**, that ye may prove what is that good and acceptable and perfect will of God."* **Ephesians 2.10 (*AMP*)**

*"For we are God's [own] handiwork (His workmanship), recreated in Christ Jesus, [born anew], that we may **do those good works** which God predestined (planned   beforehand) for us, [taking paths which He prepared ahead of time] **that we should walk in them [living the good life** which He prearranged and made ready for us to live]."*

A very substantial part of this life is realized and discovered through the preaching and teaching of the gospel. However, in many religious institutions, these Scriptures are never mentioned, causing many who *lack the faith* necessary to experience such a lifestyle to forfeit God's provision because they never heard it.

Romans 10:17 states: "So then faith cometh by hearing, and hearing by the word of God."

A Lesson from the Comics

In the comic strip, Superman, there is a depiction of a seemingly common man that allows insight into the real (spirit) man; beneath the surface and is on standby daily waiting for a crisis to arise. These situations allow him to demonstrate his uncommonly supernatural abilities among common people.

Let's look at superman. He is an extraordinarily powerful man among a class of people distinguished as super friends. Each of the super friends operated like normal ordinary citizens. Until these cataclysmic events occurred and buildings began falling, trains derailing, cars and trucks crashing and the crowds began frantically losing control.

Many people were screaming and some were fleeing without instruction, others were panic-strickened, and terrified. In the midst of the horrific noises and chaos, suddenly, the real man burst out of the calamity and began controlling, rescuing, directing, and taking charge of an out of control situation. As a whisper of wind demanded the attention of the masses, someone shouted "look! It's a bird, it's a plane, it's Superman!"

It was all, the otherwise known, Clark Kent needed. Do you remember the bumbling idiot working at the Daily Planet, stumbling around clumsily pursuing Lois Lane? Lois knew she liked him, but he never manifested anything other than nerdish tendencies, so she was uninterested. In the midst of crisis Lois is uninhibited in her enticement to the person that looks just like Superman, but the difference is he has an "S" on his chest and now instead of the problem managing him; he is now exercising dominion over the problem.

Now, the Lesson

What was the comic saying? Was he saying that the

difference between Superman and us is that when pressure comes he allows it to make him, while it breaks you? Let me tell you something, the cycle of life is on this wise; while you are having trouble with your problems, someone else is triumphing over you through them because they generate what you need in order to correct your problem. So you pay them to deal with your problems. You would drown in them if someone else didn't create a lifeline to deliver you.

The mediocre state of mind is the mind that says I can't survive without the assistance of others. Friends you must learn that there is a "greater" that lives inside of you that can turn your troubles into triumphs, your valleys into mountains, and your problems into pleasures.

Paul promises that God will not allow you to encounter more than you were built to handle. "*...But will, with the temptation* (test and trial) *also make a way to escape, that **you may be able to bear it**.*" John says that "*whatsoever is born of God overcomes the world and this is the victory that overcomes the world, even our Faith*". Many times Believers fail to properly evaluate crisis that arise in life.

Understanding Crises

Many times Believers are crippled because they fail to understand that crises in life are not unique situations designed to erode their courage or confidence. However, they are opportunities that enable Believers to demonstrate Christ, to show non-believers why it is essential to have such a strong man and strong word within.

Even the wisest, strongest, most noble and most successful patriarchs, kings, queens, presidents, scholars, and professionals have suffered chapters of heartbreak and failure. Commonly they, like us, have learned that victory does not come without valleys, power is not generated without pressure, and true gain is the result of sometimes many losses and that failure is many times the womb of success which is the price we all pay for living.

Believers who allow disappointments and defeats to dissolve their faith (trust) in God will always remain in the shadows of others, hiding behind sorry apologies and excuses while the years waste away. An anonymous writer once stated that "Success, when it comes overnight, often departs with the dawn. Therefore, failure is, in a sense, the highway to success." The Apostle Paul conveyed insights about the Believer's ability to prevail through Christ.

Paul's Perspective

In his second letter to the Corinthians Paul stated that we have a treasure within us to show that this power, ability, and light we manifest through crises is from God and not from us.

But we have this treasure in earthen vessels, that the excellency of the power may be of God, and not of us. We are troubled on every side, yet not distressed; we are perplexed, but not in despair; persecuted but not forsaken; cast down but not destroyed; always bearing about in the body the dying of the Lord Jesus that the life also of Jesus might be made manifest in our body. 2 Corinthians 4:7-10 (KJV)

Notice the Amplified

"However, we possess this precious treasure, the divine light of the Gospel, in frail, human vessels of earth that the grandeur and exceeding greatness of the power may be shown to be of God and not from ourselves. We are hedged in, pressed on every side, troubled and oppressed in every way; but not cramped nor crushed; we suffer embarrassments and are perplexed and unable to find a way out, but not driven to despair;

We are persecuted and hard driven, pursued but not deserted to stand alone; strucked down to the ground, but never struck out destroyed; Always bearing about in the body, the liability and exposure to the same putting to death that the Lord Jesus suffered. So that the resurrection life of Jesus also, may be shown forth by, and in our bodies." (2 Corinthians 4:7-10, AMP)

The thing that Paul is saying in this passage is that there is another "you" inside of you, but you've gotten so accustomed to catering to the one you see that you never expect the inner person to take over. In this case, to be mediocre means to never expect anything better than what you are already accustomed to experiencing on a daily basis.

Some people have had (just) enough bad experiences to expect bad situations to continue to occur. They only use their imagination to expect more bad experiences. Then they constantly speak death in accordance with what they imagine; conditioning themselves to live hopelessly.

Other Believers will never try to do certain things again because they have been convinced through past experiences that new methods, new systems, and new ideas won't work. These improper assessments or false evaluations carry over into too many areas of their life setting the stage for a life dominated by mediocrity.

We must realize that crisis provides opportunities for Believers, who live by faith, to manifest the ability of Christ that is within.

Satan knows that he doesn't have to send demons to disrupt many converts. There are a few people in the church that get most of the demonic activity. There are many people in the church who will never need demonic coercion; they do the devil's job for him, without any coercion or suggestion. Simultaneously, they perform demonic activities. Mediocrity here means that they have accepted things the way they are and are not open to anything new, even though the systems they employ are not effective.

Many people get satisfaction out of just having somebody they can talk to about problems they face. They sit around chatting about the latest news, never discussing even a hint of what they can do to stop it.

When new ideas and concepts are generated that has the

potential to change the situations they are tired of, they persecute them because their "limited vision" is subjected to a closed mind dominated by mediocrity.

Mediocrity cannot accept what it cannot see. This means that a blind state of mind has accepted a lie from the pit that things will not change despite attempts to make life better.

Mind Blindness

According to Paul in Ephesians 4:17 "I'm urging you to stop walking like other Gentiles walk." How did they walk? In the vanity or futility of their minds; do you know what the vanity of the mind is?

It is the mind that has never been taught what the life of God is and therefore has no conviction to prepare itself to know. It is the mind that is bent on being common with life as it was prior to the experience of salvation. It is the mind that has never believed that it can quit falling victim to the same habits.

Remember, anyone who becomes a part of a new system, society, or culture without proper orientation, will be dysfunctional and eventually disenfranchised. **Let's call it the "curse of the 3 Ds": disoriented, dysfunctional, and disenfranchised.** This description fits a large percentage of the religious community. The primary reason that some habits keeps Kingdom citizens bound is because they were never properly yoked to Christ to learn His ways. As a result, they fail to realize the power within to change through Christ. This is the primary reason Hosea said that God's people are destroyed for a lack of knowledge.

Life Without Proper Orientation

The devastation of attempting godly pursuits the wrong way!

Have you ever been in a *good* fight before? Have you ever fought a fight and lost? Many times the pain of losing teaches us not to attempt things the same way again. Especially if you learned to fear defeat before you were taught the proper way to fight. Consider this; Mediocrity had settled in as a stronghold in the mind simply because of the absence of a proper orientation of life.

Satanic and worldly reasoning infiltrated many minds, establishing improper thought patterns that through time have shaped the way the majority of our religious society functions. What has become **normal** to many is now the thing they **value**. The thing they *value* has become their **standard**. Their *standards* have constructed their **beliefs** which have shaped their **convictions** and now their *convictions* are determining their constant **responses**.

Another factor that must be included is decisiveness. Now, if you have ever run up against a real good obstacle or hurdle before and it hurt you, you learned not to do that again. The energy and reasoning it took for you to make that decision is called **decisiveness**.

It's unimportant what pushed you to the point of becoming decisive; you became decisive about it and never repeated it. After we are properly orientated, we should be decisive in asserting the power and wisdom we've gained through orientation to take control and exercise dominion over habits that dominate us.

The only thing wrong with the ugly habits someone have may exist as a result of alcohol, smoking, crack, smack, methyl, seaweed, bennies, red devils, uppers, or downers. It doesn't matter what it is, when someone is decisive and stands upon God's Word, the "ugly habit" cannot subdue you any longer.

Now, as you walk by faith in the Word, refuse to open the door to your heart and emotions any longer to negatives. If you take the instructions from the Word of God for granted, that's mediocrity—and it means you don't mind having an excuse to hide behind to use as a reason not to change. This kind of complacent thinking cripples millions of strong, educated, and gifted individuals. In the case of Believers, this type of thinking is called walking in the vanity of the mind. It is a state of mind that opposes the *truth* of God about life.

Winning Over Mediocrity by Kingdom Principles

Remember, it may be difficult in the beginning to conquer mediocrity. But it is important to remind yourself that you must persist until you succeed. You may have already tried other systems or methods to conquer bad habits but to no avail. When using kingdom principles, pay particular attention in the first few days and it is likely you will be able to identify the ills of your own life.

First, you will be able to determine *why* you have the kind of problems you do. Then, you will discover the importance of paying attention. However, be mindful that until you personally identify those things that challenge your progress, you will keep experiencing the same crisis. Commit to structuring your lifestyle in such a way that God is glorified through your obedience to His Word. Within four-to-six weeks, you will begin to experience personal growth and power. If you have a problem managing your time effectively, prioritizing your relationships, finances, and other critical areas, you will have a problem prioritizing your "triune" [three-part] man; spirit, soul, and body.

Remember, your tri-unity is prioritized by honoring your spirit-man first. If your decisions are not based on the regard of your spirit-man first, then you set yourself up for defeat. The way that you gage success through the spirit-man is to make sure that whatever the whole-man is getting ready to do, lines up with the Word of God.

The **spirit of man** is first, the **soul of man** is second, and the **body of man** is last.

Here is an example: If we implement a physical structure in our life first through exercise, our physical body will become stronger than our spirit. Because of this, a spiritual devotion *first* is imperative to prepare and equip us for our physical endeavors. We must "**commit our way to the Lord and our work shall be**

established."

Some people want to have a sound operation but they go about it in an unsound and ineffective way. The Bible says, "**First seek the Kingdom of God** and its righteousness and all these other things shall be added."

Mediocrity is a State of Mind

Why are some Believers stuck in sin, sickness, and poverty, even though the price of redemption has been paid and the Gospel emphatically proclaims our deliverance? Certainly the curse of the 3-Ds exposes many contributing factors.

The heart (spirit) must be established in faith, by the Word of God, and the mind must be prepared to attract the reality it desires from the Word. It is only after this that real change will manifest. True success in any area, especially for the inexperienced, will require continuity of thought and passionate desire that generates strong focus.

There is also a difference in wishing for a "thing" and being ready to receive that "thing." None of us are really ready for just *anything* until we believe we can acquire it. Belief is essential. A person also needs activities that connect them from day-to-day to their aspirations as well as their thoughts.

Where there are too many breaks, people tend to lose sight of their goals. This may lead to frustration and confusion. Some actually fail because too many breaks dissolved the passion and momentum they started with. Do you believe that you can acquire the promises in the Word? The Word of God proves that people whose lives hardly ever receive these promises actually disappoint and anger God (see Hebrews 3:4 and Numbers 13:14).

Noah Example

God said to Noah, "Build me an ark"... Noah asked "Why?" God replied "Because rain is coming." Noah said, "Lord I've never seen the rain." God told Noah not to worry and said, "I'll show it to you, and you just commit to building the ark ... and conform your activities to whatever it takes to manifest the ark as an earthly reality. At the appointed time you will see the rain when you are sheltered in the Ark."

The Ark of Provision

The same day that God gave Noah the promise of provision for his present crisis was the same day He gave Noah the promise of provision for his future; to secure his eternity.

Many have sadly misunderstood that the promise of faith is just as much a provision for now as it is against tomorrow's end of age. The problem some have is that they believe God has delivered them from the fires of hell through the blood of Jesus, and that they may go to Heaven. However, they do not realize that same promise that allowed Noah to escape the future damnation (the flood) was the same promise (the ark) that sustained Him during the stormy rain. In other words, the ark was filled with the abundance of God's provision.

There was not one animal on the boat that had to eat the other, neither did Noah's family eat meat. Noah believed God and moved! Noah structured his life around the promise. And as he structured his life he was able to complete the tasks God had given him.

It impacted his life, the lives of his family, and the generations that followed. So, structuring your life will potentially impact the lives of others associated with you for generations!

Let's Be Real!

Ironically, many Believers today would not believe if God said to them that they can have an uncommon blessing. Most would be so dominated by mediocre thinking and closed minds that they would likely discount it as God for the three basic reasons listed earlier. I called it "DDD"; the three crippling Ds of Christianity;

disoriented, dysfunctional, and disenfranchised.

Understanding Faith

Your faith needs to have mission when God assigns a promise to you. The reason He gives a promise is because contained within the promises are provisions. One has to structure their lives around the promise in order to access the provision within it. This provision is two-fold when accessing through true faith: First, provision is for now (the present); second, it is for later (eternity). Jesus confirms this fact in Mark 10.30: *"he shall receive a hundredfold now in this time....and in the world to come eternal life."* God has provided everything we need, yet, as a church we haven't gotten serious about accessing it.

The religious community can be lazy, complacent, disoriented, and dysfunctional at times; a system that will remain disenfranchised if it ceases to seek God for direction. Recognize that God has done for all, but all are not trying to do for themselves. Therein lies a successful tactic among the enemy's arsenal.

The Process

We are not ready for a "thing" until we believe that we can acquire that "thing." It is the state of our mind and condition of our spirit that determines whether we live in mediocrity or by faith. A person's state of mind must be one of belief not merely wishful thinking. A closed mind cannot inspire faith. It doesn't matter what is preached or taught, if your mind is closed it can't receive. Therefore, it is essentially impossible to bring it to pass because you aren't able to see it inside of you.

There are actually people who are seriously addicted to self-deception because of an unstructured lifestyle that promotes mediocrity. This may be due to their personal philosophy of life. However, they desperately need organized thoughts (structure) aligned with the Word of God to produce or manifest the things they believe for by faith.

When the right applications are made, there is no more effort needed to aim high in life to demand abundance and prosperity from life, than is required to settle for mediocrity. I've learned that "misery and poverty" cost the same amount of time and energy that success and abundance does. It is a matter of how you bargain with life and what principles you decide to engage.

The body of Christ must begin to experience and walk daily in what the Bible identifies as our inheritance. God intends for Kingdom citizens to become "*Cities on a hill that cannot be hid.*" Which actually implies that we become high stations in the earth through our commitment to Kingdom principles and that, in turn, will a attract non-believers to God, through Christ. We cannot walk out this principle with a mediocre mentality. Jesus said "*I came that you might have life and that more abundantly.*"

Chapter 5

The Fourth Master Key

Prioritizing My Tri-une or Three-part Man

"But seek ye first the Kingdom of God, and his righteousness; and all these things shall be added unto you"

Imagine that you are about to begin construction on a housing project. Where would you start? Suppose you have gotten all the materials delivered to the site, everything's scattered in bundles and heaps, but this is your first time attempting a project of this magnitude. What would you do? First thing to know is; don't panic! So, starting a critical project such as prioritizing your tri-une (or three-part) man, where will you start? How does one start such an enormous project when everything seems to be in such disarray? Again, don't panic! I will share with you how to accomplish such an important task. There is a practical way to achieve a successful construction project. It is a tested and proven system (or method) drafted from the Master Creator's manual detailing how to do things successfully. You actually need the same process that the wisdom of God employed to renovate the earth. This is discovered in Genesis chapter one.

Prioritizing my 3 part man is a Master Key to Success! The process of setting your house in order, getting things arranged like they ought to be. To structure something means to actually build or to construct something. It is made up of a number of parts arranged together. In this case I want you to think about how you were made, who made you and why. In other words, why are you here?

The three dimensions of man

There are three dimensions of humans that have to be properly structured before anyone can fully discover their God-given purpose. Those dimensions are spirit, soul and body. The spirit man, the soul man and the body (or natural man) must be structured and functioning in proper order to experience a wholesome life.

One primary reason I emphasize the term **structure** is because each day I associate with some of the most prominent and talented people in this society. Some have an abundance of potential, yet never really exploit their inherent abilities because they accept counter-intentional and dysfunctional lives. Many others never bother to take the time to look into the owner's manual (God's Holy Word) to determine how or why they were made.

From the Owner's Manual Perspective

The Bible teaches that God made all men for Himself, for His own glory. This means that you and I were not designed to decide what was best for us without our Creator's input. Each time we purchase an instrument or piece of equipment that has several different functions; we need the owner's manual to instruct us of its proper use. In this case, the owner's manual is not something written by the user, but *for* the user. It was dictated by the originator/designer of the instrument from whom we were purchased.

It is necessary to examine what the owner has to say about proper use of this instrument because when we fail to do so, we risk damaging our goods. This happens when we lack the ability to properly and affectively use what we purchased.

Another basic reason to apply structure is to identify the way God (our owner) prioritizes our three-part being and discover the part of our being He dwells in so that we can develop an intimate relationship with Him.

Man is not only what he sees, but there is more to man than what meets the natural eye. Man is a spirit that has a soul, which lives in a body. Since we are spirit-beings first, we must recognize the need to develop our spirit man first (John 6:63).

I'm sure you know several Believers who have spent countless time and energy trying to bring their bodies to submission to God's way. They fail to understand that the natural man or body is the only part of our triune man at death that will be shed as the spirit and soul returns back to God.

So many Believers focus the majority of their time, energy, and resources on natural pursuits and comforts. Rather than focusing their time, energy, and resources into spiritual development and submission to the Kingdom of God and His righteousness.

There are three steps that must be taken to properly establish the priorities of the triune man. First, the natural man (body) or *sarkinoi* must be forced into submission to the will of God to conform to whatever target or goal he tries to accomplish from the Word of God. It is safe to say; "No force, no conformance." Second, man's mind (soul) or *psuche*, which is comprised of five faculties; thoughts, feelings, intellect, will, and disposition must be renewed by using the methods from Joshua 1:8 and Psalm 1:1-3 to dictate acceptable thoughts and images that correspond with man's desired pursuits.

This is to first control the rational part of man's soul which consists of thoughts and intellect. As man does this, he must simultaneously set his affections or emotions which marinates and incubates thoughts to align or agree with God-inspired pursuits so it becomes abundant to him. This is the process of setting affections on the things above.

Thirdly, the heart (spirit) or *pneuma* must be established and allowed to function as the chief of the three-part man. Successfully completing these three critical steps will allow the triune function properly. So, what are you waiting for? You are only three steps away from a PRINCIPLE centered life!

The Natural Man Must be Forced into Submission

Romans 8.8 implies that to live according to the flesh is to live a life dominated by the dictates and desires of a sinful human nature.

The flesh here is referred to as man's *lower nature* (his body or natural mind influenced by satanic and worldly advice). Notice that "the flesh **cannot** please God.

> *So then they that are in the* **flesh** *cannot please God. But you are not in the flesh, but in the Spirit, if so be that the Spirit of God dwell in you.*

This is a very emphatic statement that factors very heavily in a Believer's ability to experience prosperity in the Kingdom of God. Since this is the case at hand, Paul insists that a life dominated by such dictates and desires leaves a person vulnerable to the *works of the flesh*, mentioned in Galatians 5:19-21, further declaring that "*they which do such things shall not inherit the Kingdom of God.*" Each of these passages outlines the necessity of body subjection. In Paul's first letter to Corinth, he explains the importance of bringing the body into compliance of God's Word to be worthy of receiving the prize.

> *Know ye not that they which run in a race run all, but one receiveth the prize? So run, that ye may obtain. And every man that striveth for the mastery is* **temperate** *in all things. Now they do it to obtain a corruptible crown; but we an incorruptible. I therefore so run,* **not as uncertainly**, *so fight I,* **not as one that beateth the air: But I keep under my body, and bring it into subjection:** *lest that by any means, when I have preached to others, I myself should be a castaway.* (1 Corinthians 9:24-27 KJV)

Here Paul compares himself to the racers and combatants in the games well known to the Corinthians. Those who ran in their games were placed on a strict diet and had to exercise extreme discipline. In Paul's mind they are the examples of how Believers should likewise abstain from fleshly appetites and heathenistic sacrifices for the heavenly crown.

Those who fought with one another in these exercises prepared themselves by beating the air, as the Apostle calls it, or by throwing out their arms and thereby injuring themselves beforehand to better prepare themselves for close combat.

There is no room for any such exercise in Christian warfare. Christians are always in close combat. Our fleshly enemies make fierce and hearty opposition and are in constant pursuit of our bondage. For this reason, Believers must remain earnest and never drop out of the contest, nor attempt to retire from it. We must fight, not as those that beat the air, but we must strive against the strongholds with all our might.

Paul mentions one contemptible enemy; the body (or the natural man). The body must be kept under, beaten black and blue (as the combatants were in the Grecian games) and constantly brought into subjection. By the "body," Paul is speaking of fleshly appetites and inclinations. Everyone who will pursue the interest of their souls must be committed to beat their bodies into compliance. They must endure hard combat against fleshly lusts until they are subdued. **The body must be made to serve the mind** as it is renewed by spiritual principles and not be allowed for a moment to lord over it.

Your Mind Must be Renewed and Your Affections set on High Things

In other words, a person's thoughts need to be tried and their feelings need weighed because of the potential deception of both. Just because a person becomes a Believer does not mean that the way they think or feel instantly becomes godly or right.

Entry into any new arena or phase of life requires proper orientation. This is true in relationships, cultural changes, professions and career paths, new equipment and upgrades in technology. This has certainly been neglected in Christianity far too long. It appears to me that if industries and corporations understand the significance of employee orientation and training before allowing new employees to operate, the Body of Christ should at least realize that new converts must be orientated and trained as well.

Importance of Orientation

It is no wonder Jesus said of the Scribes and Pharisees that they go through discomforting difficulties to get one follower only to make the person two times worst. This is spiritual assassination and should not exist in the Body of Christ. They have failed to renew their minds.

Any organization, group, club, or Church that desires to progress, expand, or grow (including personnel recruitment) must understand the priority of orientation. In most performance-based organizations, when a new employee is disoriented, they are dysfunctional in that organization and will eventually become disenfranchised. These three Ds are responsible for most of the devastation occurring in the Christian community than any other satanic implant.

Mind Renewal Begins With Orientation

Without orientation a person really does not know what to expect. They are not aware of purposes, goals, missions, policies, practices, systematic functions, or performance expectations within the new affiliation. Orientation sets the stage for the essential parts of a lesson or a task to be conveyed and grasped with less difficulty.

In these two verses Paul gives practical advice to the Believers in Rome. They should offer their bodies and *mind to prove God's will.* Paul urges the Believers at Rome to engage true worship; not as a ritual or noble act.

As the well-known commentator, William Barkley, wrote; "Real worship is the offering of everyday life to him, not something transacted in a church, but something which sees the whole world as the temple of the living God."

A person may say, I am going to church to worship God, but he should also be able to say, I'm going to work, the store, the restaurant, to the park, the game, the neighbors house, the mall, and anywhere else he goes to worship God. After orientating the Romans with an earnest discussion about reasonable service to open their minds, Paul begins to demand radical change. Why? Because he knew that a Godly message could not be effectively communicated to a closed natural mind.

And be not conformed to this world: but be ye transformed by **the renewing of your mind***, that ye may prove what is that good, and acceptable and perfect will of God.*

To express this idea he uses two, almost untranslatable, Greek words; *suschemati-zesthai,* which means to be conformed to this world. The root of this word is *schema;* meaning the outward form that varies from day-to-day and year-to-year.

Barkley writes "A man's *schema* is not the same when he is fifteen-years-old as it is when he is fifty. It is not the same when he goes out to work as it is when he is dressed for dinner; it is continuously altering. So Paul says, "Don't try to match your life to all the fashions of this world; don't be like a chameleon which takes its color from its surroundings."

The word he uses for being transformed from the world is *metamorphousthai.* Its root is *morphe,* which means the essential unchanging shape or element of a thing. A man has not the same schema at fifteen and fifty, but he has the same *morphe.* A man in blue jeans has not the same *schema* as a man in evening attire but they have the same *morphe.* His outward form changes, but inwardly he is the same person. So, Paul says, to worship and serve God, we must undergo a change, not of our outward form but of our inward personality. What is this change?

Paul would say that left to ourselves we live a life of *kata sarka,* dominated by human nature at its lowest. In Christ we live a life of *kata Christon* or *kat pneuma,* dominated by Christ or by the Spirit. The essential man has been changed. Now, he lives, not a self-centered but, a Christ-centered life. This must happen by the renewal of his mind.

The Word he uses for renewal is *anakainosis*. In Greek there are two words for "new"--*neos* and *kainos*. *Neos* means new in point of time; *Kainos* means new in point of character and nature. A newly manufactured pencil is *neos*, but a man who was once a sinner and is now on his way to being a saint is *kainos*. When Christ comes into a man's life he is a new man; his mind is different, because the mind of Christ is in him.

When Christ becomes the center of a person's life then this person can present real worship, which is the offering of every moment and every action to God. According to Romans 8:5-8, an un-renewed mind leaves a Believer in limbo because the focus of the mind submits the body to what it serves. Until a man's mind is renewed he is subject to many shifts.

*For they that are after the flesh do **mind** the things of the flesh; but they that are after the Spirit the things of the Spirit. For to be **carnally minded** is death; but to be **spiritually minded** is life and peace. Because the carnal mind is enmity against God: for it is not subject to the law of God, neither indeed can be. So then they are in the flesh cannot please God.*

As I draw a contrast between the two kinds of life, notice, that there is a life dominated by sinful human nature, whose focus and center is *self*. There is a life dominated by the Spirit of God, that is **Spirit controlled** and **Christ dominated**. These two lives are going in diametrically opposite directions. The first is pointed daily towards death; the latter is steadily progressing towards God each day. Like Enoch who walked with God and God took him.

God's will is that man has the mind of Christ *Let this mind be in you, which was also in Christ Jesus: who being in the form of God, thought it not robbery to be equal with God: (Philippians 2:5, 6, KJV)*

In closer examination of 1 Corinthians 9.25-27, the Apostle Paul emphatically states the importance of self-control in striving for mastery. He urges the Believer to develop the fruit of *temperance* in all things.

*"And every man that strives for the mastery is **temperate** in all things. Now they do it to obtain a corruptible crown but we are incorruptible.*

I have already discussed how athletes who pursue natural crowns and accomplishments will do whatever it takes to become achievers. This selective group of aspiring men and women willingly forsake family, natural pleasures, and many other daily distractions for the sake of obtaining a gold medal.

Several years ago in desperate pursuit of the gold medal, young figure skater, Tanya Harding injured another contestant, Nancy Kerrigan, who was projected to win the gold. Even though this rare example illustrates how the wrong focus on competing generates a lack of focus on personal development and preparation. Tanya's inability to structure and focus on the goal at hand forced her to resort to unthinkable measures to win the gold. Instead of putting her best foot forward, she tried eliminating her competitor instead of applying determination, preparation, and discipline. However, there are heaps of heroic Olympic stories demonstrating triumph and victory reflecting the *"power of temperance."*

Paul said, they do it (self-discipline, temper) to obtain a corruptible crown but, we must do it to receive an incorruptible crown. God promises that each of us, who will diligently prepare ourselves through faith, to trust in Him with all our hearts, in spite of what we must overcome, will receive the favor and goodness of the Lord. That is why Believers should spend time each day ensuring that all of their practices, systems, and operations are structured according to God's Word.

The seven components listed below, if applied consistently, enables Believers to experience godliness resulting in wholesome and successful living. These components establish the spirit as the dominant part of man

The Seven Components to Structure

1. Pray Always (ask, supplicate, intercede, give thanks)
2. Seek the Kingdom's way first (study, meditate on Scriptures)

3. Walk in Love (imitate Christ's character, obey commands, believe that God's way is best)
4. Walk by Faith (trust God's Word in *all* things)
5. Walk in the Spirit (obey God's Word despite difficulty)
6. Live in Self-denial (avoid offense, exalt others, reckon yourself "dead to self" but "alive in Him")
7. Be fruitful (commit to live as a fruitful godly character to win souls)

I'm praying for your discovery

As we continue to explore 1 Corinthians 9:25-27, concentrating on *temperance* as the focal point, I pray you begin to recognize and accept God's will and purpose for your life. There is tremendous fulfillment in purposeful, goal-driven living. Paul says that athletes and competitors have goals, aspirations, and chief aims that are worth buffeting their bodies and forsaking many loved ones. Jesus said that when a man truly loves Him he will *"forsake all to follow him."* It's amazing how people are simply not effective because they don't have a chief aim or definite purpose in life that is aligned with God's word.

Those who discover the need for purpose have something to conform to and structure their lives around. Without a chief aim or a central purpose you become subject to defeat and confusion frequently. Those with a chief aim shoot at specific targets. They are never satisfied hitting the things around the target. Nothing, but the bull's-eye, which is their chief aim, will satisfy them.

This is another reason so many persons struggle day-after-day with keeping devotional periods and daily reading consistent Bible study and confessions of Scripture that generate faith and develop character. This is simply because of the absence of a chief aim or a defined purpose. Jesus said, *"If you love me you will keep my commandments."* The right emotion and thought (which is love) will generate the right action in response to the right information.

The developing of plans, ideas, and concepts successfully requires continuity of thought and passionate desire that generates strong focus combined with a commitment to constant application. For example, an artist progresses as far as time permits each day, until the ideas captivated in the photo-static membrane of his or her mind are fully depicted upon the canvas.

The Process

THOUGHT: As an artist, I begin with the end in mind, the place where all plans must begin. Thought and imagination are the functions of the mind that gives us the ability to see the end or final result of a thing. The only true place that allows an individual to accurately plot the steps of accomplishment is his mind. "His mind must conceive it and believe it, if he is to achieve it."

PLAN: He selects the tools necessary to accomplish his desire and organizes them. Then he estimates the amount of time needed, prepares the canvas, mixes the colors and sets the time to begin.

ACTION: His burning desire to portray the image that is so indelibly imprinted on his mind is the driving force that interlinks his thoughts and talents from day-to-day until he sees his desire accomplished.

Day after day, the artist's *goal,* which is the image *inside* of him, *ignites* passion and desire which *motivates* his *attitude,* and *stimulates* his *talent* into manipulating and creating contour and color, depth and light and collages and forms that draw him closer to completion each day.

In spite of distractions, problems that may arise, or even setbacks, his ability to stay focused on the image inside will enable him to persevere unto completion.

Here are three tips that will assist you in accomplishing your God-given, word-tested desires.

1. **Thought continuity** and connection from day-to-day

links your ideas and concepts together.

2. **Too many breaks** will cause you to lose sight of what
    you are developing. This may result in frustration and
    confusion and make it a challenge to restart or know
    where to begin again. Allowing too many breaks between
    starting and completing can lead to failure.

Anyone attempting to climb, risk the possibility of a fall but to
exist in an environment where there is no attempt is to exist where
falling is inevitable and becomes common practice. This is
unacceptable! Expect obstacles.

Air Beaters

Now, who actually beats at the air? Simply put, people who
do what they do without the proper components of duty are those
who beat at the air. Duty must be present in order to sustain the
passion and motivation needed to accomplish the underlined
objective. Don't just swing for the sake of swinging; stop showing
up at church on Sunday just for the sake of being there. Refuse to
sing in the choir just to show how good you are!

Listen, bad and anointed are distinctly different. A person
who has a chief aim, commitment, and desire to work for the Lord
to further His cause and purpose usually loves the work they do
and are "*joy generators.*" These are the ones that God will anoint.
But those who neglect to search for deeper purposes than
association and occupancy (those who perform without defined
purpose) will work as hard, if not harder, without fulfillment and
without anointing.

Example

I will never forget the many experiences of my teen years in
various choirs and the teaching ministry that allowed me to
witness how time, temptation, and trouble would always test and
determine the type of people we were partnering with. These types

of people are usually singing just to be singing in the choir. Yet they never transfer the songs or the motivation of the song into their personal lives. In a short period of time they might experience a loss of excitement, run out of fuel, and eventually deteriorate in their commitment leading them into sporadic attendance prior to quitting. We *all* need a sense of purpose about why we do what we do. We also need a chief aim. Chief aims enable us to focus regardless of the distractions that are sure to come.

A meaningful struggle in context

Why is it so hard for individuals to structure their lives? It's difficult because those individuals have lived without structure for so long. It's very hard for dysfunctional individuals to manifest a reality externally that they have never envisioned or imagined internally. It's also very difficult for people to commit to a transitional lifestyle when it has never been a part of their daily routine.

Most of us adapt to things that don't require much change rather smoothly. It's easier to get involved in something that is similar to what you are already apart of, even though, in many cases this too is a hard task. The key here is that we need a chief aim, a goal that gives us purpose. If we never establish a definite purpose we will never have a reason to structure our lives. It really should be difficult for anyone to settle for mere existence. That's mediocrity!

Psalms 1:1-3 list five basic steps that are structured to manifest prosperity in the lives of Believers who conform to its simplified demands.

Blessed is the man that ****walketh*** *not in the counsel of the ungodly, nor* ****standeth*** *in the way of the sinners, nor* ****sitteth*** *in the seat of the scornful. But his* ****delight*** *is in the law of the Lord: and in his law doth he* ****meditate*** *day and night. And he shall be like a tree planted by the rivers of water, that bringeth forth his fruit in his season; his leaf also shall not wither; and whatsoever he doeth shall prosper. (Psalm 1:1-3)*

Notice that this is not a quick fix but a process that must be walked out through time. Life is a process, not an event. Those who really need immediate or swift results wear out fast, or they burn out quick. Since they think they need to see physical or material evidence before they get started, they are usually very easily discouraged.

While each of the five steps are important, step one is the most pivotal step. Step one reflects the necessity of steps four and five. Let's call these steps "the structured lifestyle of the blessed."

Structured Lifestyle of the Blessed:

Step 1. Does not seek or accept ungodly counsel (advice,

Information)

Step 2. Does not stand where sinners stand

Step 3. Does not sit in scorn

Step 4. His delights and desires are in the law of God

Step 5. He meditates in that law day and night

A recovering addict once commented "I went to church every Wednesday and every Sunday for a solid month and nothing happen. I'll be honest with you; I gave it my all, so I'm not going back. If God was going to do anything for me he would have done it then, because I was more faithful then than I have ever been in all my life. In fact, I didn't sin for that month; I told no lies, I paid all my bills, and I did not try any of my former habits that month. You think God cared? No, not at all! God did nothing to help me."

For this reason the Bible teaches that, "*in your patience you possess your soul.*" Hebrews 10:36 states "*for you have need of patience, that after you have done the will of God, ye might receive the promise.*" Today's society has progressed into a quick fix; hurry up, fast-food system that serves up the product of desire without the proper ingredients needed to sustain the good produced.

The cost is premium, but the quality is poor. Seemingly, these type entities have nurtured the idea that life is an event where one miracle will happen and everyone will ride off into the sunset, healthy, wealthy, and wise. Life is not an event. Life is a process! This process requires focus, diligence, knowledge, wisdom, hard work and many other virtues that bring peace and wholesomeness. What we must realize is that the spirit-man prioritizes life totally different than the soul and physical-man (natural) man does. Remember, man is a *tripartite* or (three-part being). What makes man effective is when there is an emergence between all three personalities (spirit, soul, and body) based upon godly or spiritual reasoning while the spirit man is the controller.

What makes man a negative presence that works against himself that his body or (natural-man) is dominated by worldly information and merges with his soul-man without the priority of the spirit-man empowered by Kingdom or spiritual knowledge and wisdom? Realize that whomever the soul-man merges with (between natural and spiritual) becomes the dominant expression and reigning chief of our being.

Some people have no sense of purpose because the appetite of their body determines every place they go and everything they do. For instance, they leave the Sunday worship service without devising a system that will enable reflection on the message preached. So, in desperation they need a meal, a smoke, some form of entertainment, or fellowship immediately. This is an early indication that their body is in control of their soul and therefore ruling the whole man.

This practice silences the spirit part of your triune man and rules the whole man. The silencing of the spirit part of your tri-unity subjects the whole man to hardship, stresses, and many unnecessary exchanges that could be avoided.

So what you have to do is learn how to prioritize life through the filters of the spirit-man. This begins with proper *Hearing* which I will address later. But in this case my emphasis is to properly discern. In Mark 4:23-34, Jesus said, *"If any man has ears to hear, let him hear. And he said unto them, take heed what you hear."* In other words, what or whom you listen to can seriously determine your success or failure.

The Power of Advice

Note in Psalms 1:1 that the word *counsel* there means *advice.* *"Blessed is the man who walketh not in the counsel of the ungodly."* The Amplified says, *"Blessed happy, fortune, prosperous and enjoyable is the man who walks and lives not in the counsel of the ungodly."*

In other words, to follow ungodly advice, to follow their plans, or to follow their purposes is tragic. But, godly advice is profitable and necessary in all things, and at all times.

During the early months of summer I noticed that I had actually slipped back into a pattern of attracting time wasters and distracters that were causing me great frustrations because I was being hindered from completing important tasks. One morning while praying, the Holy Spirit directed me to visit a good friend who lives a very structured and highly productive life. I left church immediately to solicit his assessment of my situation. As I entered his store I observed him very cautiously moving across the floor aware of his customers but focused on finishing his task.

"Hi Bro!" I said, reluctantly, (not wanting to impose). "I need your input on something briefly if you can spare a few minutes." "Sure," He replied. We entered his office and sat down, and I began laying out my frustrations. Looking straight into my eyes as an intense physician would, he replied! "Pastor Bush, **your value is determined by the amount of problems you solve for others, not by how many people you listen to.** In your position as the senior leader of the church the majority of your time must not be spent on the least priorities or small fires that subordinates can resolve, because **people, who don't respect your time, won't respect your wisdom!**" Although, He shared many other prudent tips that day, these two highlighted statements helped me to initiate changes that enabled me to become more effective and get back on track.

Notice, after clarifying the power of advice the Psalmist continues; *"Nor stands submissive and inactive in the path where sinner walk, nor sits down to relax and rest where the scornful and the mockers gather; but **his delight and desire** are in the law of the Lord and on his law the precepts, the instructions, the teachings of God he habitually meditates, (he ponders and studies) by day and by night and **he shall be like a tree firmly planted** by and tended by the streams of water ready to bring forth his fruits in its season, his leaf also shall not fade or wither and **everything he does** shall prosper."*

I can't promise you prosperity any other way, but God's way. We are blessed if we refuse to walk in the counsel of the ungodly. Now, the Word of God distinctly tells us how we should eat, it tells us the proper way to rest, the proper way to manage money, the proper way to maintain health, what our relationships ought to look like, how we should conduct ourselves on the job, how our marriages should be structured, and how Kingdom parenting should be conducted.

It tells us when and how to purchase, how to build a house, how to redeem our time, and how to walk in the spirit. It tells us everything we need to know in order to be effective in gathering Kingdom inheritance in our earthly life. In fact Proverbs 4.26 implies that there is an established route for success in every endeavor. *"Ponder the path of thy feet, and let all thy ways be established."* (KJV)

Another view of Psalms 1:1 is that the most ungodly advice you will hear will come from within you! Nobody will talk to you about doing the evil, selfish, foolish, insensitive, sinful, hurtful, harmful, lustful, and wicked deeds that you will do like Satan and your untrained "self".

Most people are afraid to tell you to go and get sloppy drunk and make a fool of yourself. The majority certainly would not dare tell you to rob a bank. Regardless of how a person may feel or think about you, most would not assume the liberty to suggest extreme activities unless you are partners in some type of conspiracy or plan together. It's true! We as humans give ourselves some very wicked counsel.

How Information Gets in the Mix

Believers and non-believers must realize that the problem is not we, it's me! The problem isn't what others say to us, it is what we say to ourselves after we hear it. What God is trying to convey through the psalmist is that our ungodly nature gets the best of us when empowered by ungodly counsel. Ungodly counsel (words we hear) both internal and external are destructive forces. Dr. Myles Munroe once stated that *"wisdom protects us from the dangers of knowledge."* Certainly, we need the wisdom of God as a filter for all incoming information.

When we listen to ungodly counsel, we fuel the ungodly part of our tripartite which is considered fleshly or carnal. When we listen to godly counsel we fuel our *spirit part*. The abundance of what we listen to actually develops or determines the functions and reasoning of our soul part. This ultimately influences the activities and responses of our body.

When information influences our thoughts and emotions, if it is allowed to reside while compounding with similar sorts, it will determine the posture (will or attitude) of the *soul part* of our tri-unity. The Apostle Paul says in Romans 8:5 that **the fixed state of our mind will determine the course of our walk.** *"For they that are after the flesh do **mind** the things of the flesh; but they that are after the Spirit the things of the Spirit."*

In the Gospel of Matthew 12:34-35 Jesus said, *"From the abundance of the heart the mouth speaks* (is influenced)." (KJV) The Amplified states, *"For out of the fullness, the overflow, the superabundance of the heart the mouth speaks. The good man from his **inner good treasure*** *flings forth good things, and the evil man out of his **inner evil store house** flings forth evil things. Notice, the implication here is that life does not just happen to us, but our quality of living comes from within us.*

The Apostle also warned the Corinthians of the danger of receiving from improper sources; "Do not be so deceived and misled! Evil companionships, (communion, associations) corrupt and deprave good manners and morals and character." (1Corinthians 15:33, AMP)

Clearly these scriptures enable us to understand why the Holy Spirit impressed upon the psalmist the steps necessary to empower the spirit-man as the reigning chief of the triune man and establish the heart (soul) in the Kingdom of God system.

My Rule of Thumb

Things to remember regarding the use of each "structure" ingredient.

1. Work out your own salvation by discovering the principles that will navigate you through prearranged paths that God made ready for us ahead of time that we should walk in them living according to his will. This process is called "laboring to enter into his rest"

2. The Kingdom of God consist of straight gates and narrow ways that are designed to put new converts back in right relationship with God, which results in a life of rest and peace.

3. Entering the Kingdom means to realign your life and its issues after receiving salvation (*soteria*), which initiates the deposit of abundant life.

4. Realignment of issues requires "mind renewal." You must think differently to become different.

5. Mind renewal requires prayerful Bible study, research, constant hearing, confessing the Word, daily meditating the Word, and pondering the path of your feet. Observing closely your conduct and relationships, so that your ways may progressively be reestablished to represent your Kingdom citizenship.

6. Acknowledge that many of your ways (habits, beliefs, convictions, and responses) that seemed right continue to end in destruction, thus making your situations worst. *These must be put on the hit list for change!*

7. Accepting that if your present established beliefs, habits, and responses to a particular issue do not yield peace, joy, and righteousness combined to produce wholesome living, your approach or practice regarding that issue is not producing God's best.

8. God's righteousness through Scriptures is designed to reprove, correct, and instruct you into His perfect will to secure for you a well-balanced and wholesome life.

9. Remember God's thoughts and ways are not like ours, but He gave us His word and His Spirit to bridge the gap and give us rest.

10. Your best example is Jesus; the expressed image of God.

"*He always did those things that pleased the father.*" God wants each of us to gain mastery over ourselves through Kingdom principles which are designed to enlighten and empower successful living in every area of our lives. Remember you have the Holy Spirit living inside of you to help and guide you daily.

In the Kingdom of God the roads have been mapped out and the way paved, so I invite you to take this adventurous journey by using these ingredients of structure and your life will become more purposeful and fulfilling each day!

Chapter 7

The Use of Laws and Principles

Remember that as you journey, your regard and honor for principles must be heighten to a level that allows you to always know that Laws and principles have no greater respect for a crawling infant or toddler just beginning to walk than for a senior citizen turning one-hundred-years-old.

If either were actually taken to a sixteen story roof and allowed to wonder beyond the edge, they would experience a deadening fall that would probably be regarded as something God allowed or simply something God planned. But neither explanation would stand up against the truth.

Truth is the laws and principles that govern life do not respect the ignorant, intelligent, or disobedient, no more than the obedient, unless they adhere to their existence. Ignorance of the laws and principles does not change their demands. I have yet to see the law of gravity change its nature to respect any force weaker than itself.

Only when a higher law is initiated, does the reigning law yield! As in the case of the law of gravity which is always a force to reckon with in the earth-realm versus the law of thrust. Even though, what goes up must come down, whenever the rate of speed is accomplished within an accelerated span of time, the law of thrust super seeds the law of gravity because gravity now yields to it.

In order for you to overcome the way of fleshly nature you must walk in the spirit. This is clearly what the apostle Paul meant in Romans 8:2, 3, "***For the law of the Spirit of life in Christ Jesus has made me free from the law of sin and death***. *For what the law could not do in that it was weak through the flesh, God did by sending His own Son in the likeness of sinful flesh, on account of sin: He condemned sin in the flesh, that the righteous requirement of the law might be fulfilled in us who do* *not walk according to the flesh but according to the Spirit."* Here James also states *"It is not the hearers of the law that are just before God, but the doers who shall be justified."*

Let's Get Conscious about Setting our Attitude Right Once and for All

The time has come when we can no longer afford to have conflicting feelings about our response to foundational things. The feeling of ambivalence has dominated the operation of many confused, disinterested, and ignorant Believers resulting in the appearance of "brokenness without remedy."

The Demand for Structured Discipline

It is the difference between *the hard and the easy way*. There is never an "easy way" to greatness; greatness is always the product of toil. Hesiod, the old Greek poet, writes, "Wickedness can be had in abundance easily; smooth is the road, and very nigh she dwells; but in front of virtue the gods immortal have put sweat." Epicharmus said, "The gods demand of us toil as the price of all good things." "Knave," he warns, "Yearn not for the soft things, lest thou earn the hard."

William Barkley gives this account in his Bible commentary on what it takes to develop discipline for success: "Once, Edmund Burke made a great speech in the House of Commons. Afterwards his brother Richard Burke was observed in deep thought. He was asked what he was thinking about, and answered, "I have been wondering how it has come about that Ned has contrived to monopolize all the talents of our family; but then again I remember that **when we were at play, he was always at work.**"

Even when a thing is done with an appearance of ease, that ease is the product of unremitting toil. The skill of the master executants on the piano, or the champion player on the golf course did not come without sweat. There never has been any other way to greatness than the way of toil, and anything else which promises such a way is a delusion and a snare.

It is the difference between *the disciplined and the undisciplined way. Nothing was ever achieved without discipline;* and many an athlete and **many a man has been ruined because he abandoned discipline and let himself grow slack.** Coleridge is the supreme tragedy of his indiscipline. Never did so great a mind, produce so little.

He left Cambridge University to join the army; he left the army because, in spite of all his erudition, he could not rub down a horse; he returned to Oxford and left without a degree. He began a paper called *The Watchman* which lived for ten numbers (100 years) and then died. It has been said of him: "He lost himself in *visions of work to be done,* that always remained to be done. Coleridge had every poetic gift but one-the gift of sustained and concentrated effort."

In his head and in his mind he had all kinds of books, as he said, himself, "completed save for transcription." "I am on the eve, "he says, "of sending to the press two octavo volumes." **But the books were never composed outside Coleridge's mind; because he would not face the *discipline* of sitting down to write them out.** No one ever reached any eminence, and no one having reached it ever maintained it, without discipline." (Barklay)

The Importance of Structured Disciplines

Proverbs 16:32, *He that is slow to anger is better than the mighty; and he that ruleth his spirit than he that taketh a city.*

Here wisdom has determined it as vitally necessary for the twenty-first century Kingdom citizen to have the grace of meekness and self-discipline. Grace that will assist all Believers in learning important lessons, navigating their course successfully, and in making proper adjustments during these difficult times that are now upon us.

To effectively communicate the importance of today's Believers developing consistent character, I chose this passage because here, a person's priority is to be *slow to anger*, not easily offended, put into passion, nor apt to resent provocation. But he or she must take time to consider before engaging others with-out-of-control outbreaks.

This tempered citizen is so slow in their motions towards anger that they may be quickly stopped and put to ease. One who "rules" as if in control of every increment on the scale of their character may respond appropriately.

It is to have the rule of **our own spirits, appetites, affections,** and all our **inclinations,** but particularly our **passions,** and **anger,** keeping them under direction and check.

In other words, as Christians we are to rule or be lords over our anger as God demonstrates throughout the Scriptures. We must be *lords of our anger,* as God is, spoken of in Nahum 1:3, Notice, *"The Lord is slow to anger, and great in power."* Ephesians 4:26, admonishes that we *"Be angry and sin not."*

Next, notice the honor of such meekness. He that gets and keeps the mastery of his passions *is better than the mighty,* better *than he that takes a city.* Such a person is acknowledged as greater than Alexander or César who were both responsible for great conquest.

The conquest of self and our own unruly passions require more true wisdom and a more steady, constant, and regular management than obtaining a victory over the forces of an enemy or controlling the lives of others.

We who are slow to anger understand that to represent God means to demonstrate only His character in times of testing: *"When a man's ways please the LORD, He makes even his enemies to be at peace with him."* (Proverbs 16:7)

Believers who are Slow to Anger are far better than the Mighty

A second mention of this quality that speaks mainly to the disadvantage of undisciplined living is also found in Proverbs 25:28, "He that *hath* no rule over his own spirit *is like* a city *that is* broken down, *and* without walls."

While the person that has *rule over his own spirit* maintains the government of himself, and of his own appetites and passions, he does not suffer them to rebel against reason and conscience. He has the rule of his own thoughts, his desires, his inclinations, his resentments, and keeps them all in order. He learns wisely how to interact with others by examining closely the difficult challenge of managing himself.

In contrast the man who has no rule over his own spirit who, when temptations are before him, has no government of himself. When he is offended or provoked he breaks out into unrestrained, misguided passions, which causes him to appear "*like a city that is broken down and without walls.*"

His failure to prioritize the development of systems and methods to assist him in ruling himself, have left him exposed to the temptations of Satan. Such a person becomes an easy prey to that diabolical enemy who constantly brings assaults against his assignment, leaving him liable to many troubles and vexations.

Years ago, I had to acknowledge as a leader that attempting to reconstruct a life is a very difficult challenge. Many times we focus on the secondary rather than the primary. Leading others is secondary, leading ourselves is primary.

I desperately needed to go through the process of gaining mastery over my own personal struggles if I was to succeed in assisting others with their struggles. Like the Apostle Paul, I had to learn how to "*keep my body disciplined, to bring it into subjection; for fear that after proclaiming the things pertaining to the gospel to others. I myself should become unfit, and be rejected as a counterfeit.*"

Constant introspection and self honesty enabled me to realize that God provides leadership for us by the Holy Spirit. However, it is our responsibility to use His Word to train and discipline ourselves to remain fit to be led as His witnesses.

Jesus promised in the gospel of John 8:32-33, *"Then Jesus said to those Jews who believed Him, "If you abide in My word, you are My **disciples** indeed. And you shall know the truth, and the truth shall make you free."*

Friends there are hundreds of "if's" in the Bible which are conditional and require specific responses in order to enjoy its benefits. This is a primary reason to start exercising and practicing His righteousness today. Even the Apostle Paul acknowledges that to live without discipline frustrates the empowerment of the Holy Spirit.

Striving for a Crown

*"Do you not know that those who run in a race all run, but one receives the prize? **Run in such a way that you may obtain it.** And everyone who competes for the prize is **temperate in all things.** Now they do it to obtain a perishable crown, but we for an imperishable crown. Therefore I run thus: not with uncertainty. Thus I fight: not as one who beats the air. But **I discipline my body** and bring it into subjection, lest, when I have preached to others, I myself should become disqualified."* (1 Corinthians 9:24-28, NKJV)

YOU must UNDERSTAND the importance of "VISION"

"Where there is no vision [no redemptive revelation of God], the people perish; but he who keeps the law [of God, which includes that of man] --blessed (happy, fortunate, and enviable) is he."

Chapter 8

The Fifth Master Key

Discovering Destiny through Vision

Then the LORD answered me and said: "**Write the vision and make it plain on tablets, that he may run who reads it.** For the vision is yet for an appointed time; But at the end it will speak, and it will not lie. Though it tarries, wait for it; because it will surely come, it will not tarry. "Behold the proud, His soul is not upright in him; But the just shall live by his faith. **Hab. 2:2-4**

Clearly the emphasis of Proverbs 29:18 suggests that any person, family, group, organization, government system, or society that is without "vision" is destined to perish.

Vision must serve as the **internal filtration device** through which you use to make pertinent decisions, determine your priorities, establish daily activities or necessary duties, and respond to all of your shifting circumstances and unanticipated challenges on a regular basis.

It also acts as a default mechanism that enables you to consistently decide what will impact the flow of your life and ability so you are always able to continue mounting progress.

In other words, vision will help you be specific about the type of persons, activities, habits, environments, rest and diet along with other significant functions that should be a part of your life. This is the primary reason I refer to vision as **the Cornerstone to a prosperous life.** It is as Webster's New World Dictionary defined it; the basic, essential, or most important part of the foundation.

The Cornerstone to a Prosperous Life

In the Gospel of Matthew 7:24-27 Jesus said, *"These words I speak to you are not incidental additions to your life, homeowner improvements to your standard of living. They are foundational words, words to build a life on. If you work these words into your life, you are like a smart carpenter who built his **house on solid rock**. Rain poured down, the river flooded, a tornado hit—but nothing moved that house. It was fixed to the rock.*

"But if you just use my words in Bible studies and don't work them into your life, you are like a stupid carpenter who built his house on the sandy beach. When a storm rolled in and the waves came up, it collapsed like a house of cards."

Again in Matthew 12:13-17, *"Now when Jesus went into the region of Caesarea Philippi, He asked His disciples, Who do people say that the Son of Man is? And they answered, some say John the Baptist; others say Elijah; and others Jeremiah or one of the prophets. He said to them, but who do you [yourselves] say that I am? Simon Peter replied, you are the Christ, the Son of the living God.*

*Then Jesus answered him, Blessed (happy, fortunate, and to be envied) are you, Simon Bar-Jonah. For flesh and blood [men] have not **revealed** this to you, but My Father Who is in heaven. And I tell you, you are Peter [Greek, Petros--a large piece of rock], and **on this rock** [Greek, petra—a huge rock like Gibraltar] I will build My church, and the gates of Hades (the powers of the infernal region) shall not overpower it [or be strong to its detriment or hold out against it]. I will give you the keys of the kingdom of heaven; and whatever you bind (declare to be improper and unlawful) on earth must be what is already bound in heaven; and whatever you loose (declare lawful) on earth must be what is already loosed in heaven*

It is clear from the teaching of scriptures that Jesus the son of God who died for the sins of the world is the Chief-corner stone to life. But to progress in life as a wholesomely fulfilled individual either naturally or spiritually requires sight (natural) or faith (spiritual). Here faith must become to your spirit-man what your eyes are to your natural-man. *"For we walk by faith [we regulate our lives and conduct ourselves by our conviction or belief respecting man's relationship to God and divine things, with trust and holy fervor; thus we walk] not by sight or appearance."* 2 Cor. 5:7Amp

As children of God we are given the opportunity to **"Live an Expectation Driven Reality!"** But we must refuse to have *sight* without *vision!* Sight is the limited function of your lower nature; vision is the eye of faith (spiritual sight) that gives it immediate substance to *God appointed realities.* Without vision faith is blind and stagnant because it has no object to hope for or nothing to look forward to.

God appointed realities are offspring's of prophecies, promises, or merely words from God that when revealed to us birth desire or aspirations that cause us to hunger for their attainment or manifestation. This is "righteous hunger" the kind of hunger Jesus said it is a blessing to have. But as you acquire this hunger you must be swift to write it down (record it) and make it plain for your pursuit.

In John 12:16 of The Message states *"The disciples **didn't notice the fulfillment of many Scriptures at the time***, but after Jesus was glorified, they remembered that **what was written about him matched what was done to him.** "* Notice how the Scripture identified his strict adherence and conformance to what was written about Him.

Now let's compare this account with His address to Peter in verses 36-38. *"Simon Peter asked, 'Master, just where are you going?' Jesus answered, 'You can't now follow me where I'm going. You will follow later. Master,' said Peter, 'why can't I follow now? I'll lay down my life for you! Really? You'll lay down your life for me? **The truth is that before the rooster crows, you'll deny me three times.** "* These two accounts enable us to see that there is a difference in seeing and knowing, or looking and seeing. Dr. Myles Monroe once said, "Many look but few see".

True God inspired vision demands that we live an

expectation-driven reality. Keep in mind that, there are **two realities** that make up **life**; the one **you see** and the one **God says**. The first is **natural [limited]**, the latter is **spiritual [unlimited]**. Vision is born from **God's supernatural words** called "**Truth**" which is the "**ultimate reality**".

Through vision you see tomorrow today! First, your beliefs must be based upon the **Word of faith** not what you see or sense. Because if you continue to base your beliefs on sense knowledge, eventually everything becomes a problem and a threat to the security spiritual stability as Believers. Many Believers who fail to make this transition continue to walk by sight and live offended lives with good reasons.

Next, you must realize that sight usually relates to a thing according to its appearance, vision-filled faith relates to things as God intended them to be. This is why we must meditate and spend time with God.

Through meditation or muttering the mind is given the opportunity to handle words until they are transmuted into pictures. Since we see in pictures, we gain concept when we are able to change a feeling or a word into a thought or image.

The more time we spend with this exchange the more intense our passion for its reality becomes. Thus the image progresses into an imagination and from this a motion picture is born within us that now houses a procedural grace which makes what was difficult to accomplish or attain now an easy transition. Now, the reality is indelibly imprinted on the internal canvas of your mind. **You must write your "vision" down!**

Until you transcribe your vision so that you can see it on paper and begin laboring with it daily to develop a relationship with it, what you desire will be meaningless in your daily pursuits. When we can see through *spiritual vision*, better than our *natural senses* then we can prove through mind *transformation* what the *perfect will of GOD* is. This is why Paul said it is urgent that we renew our minds in Romans 12:1, 2.

I arrived at this point after many years of allowing either Satan or my ignorance to lead me into accepting good people, good things, and mediocre situations over a great life. Today, I live a great life, a life of purpose, peace, and daily fulfillment. Yesterday, even though I was genuinely born again, my life had no distinct purpose, no real direction, no continuity or flow.

As I'll describe later in each of the structured disciplines that became inclusive ingredients in the reconstructing of my new life, I was very active, busy, and helpful but not fulfilled. While making this acknowledgment of my own personal misery, the Holy Spirit said to me *"the absence of vision driven by corresponding action is the reason many people are miserable"*.

I had to learn that I was categorically a "busy-procrastinator" who like so many others was deceived by my own heart. The way to true life is straight and narrow; few are they who find it. It is a life that one must press to enter because of the many adversaries that are cosmic, self-made, and decision driven. Vision is a daring call to be different because it demands that you conform to your unique design and God-given purpose.

It is a well-spring to life from which all other meaningful and purposeful activity flows. Years ago, during my first ten years of Pastoral ministry leading as a pastor was relatively easy for me. I had good people skills and very high tolerance for almost everyone that came into the ministry. Growth was also easy because the primary focus was love and acceptance without demand for change.

But, eventually I grew weary of this type of climate because I found myself catering to demands that did not match the demands and convictions that God had placed upon my life. These were the things and the original purpose that I knew God had called me to fulfill.

As time progressed I grew to where non-functioning leaders and position holders who seemed to relish "titles" but not satisfy their positional demands could not be tolerated at all. In fact I developed a "no tolerance" agitation for those who were aware of their deficiency but did nothing to change or grow to conform to positional expectations.

Matthew 15:14 and 23:16-26 (NKJV) gave me the insight that reinforced my decision because it made me aware of how "blind guides or blind leaders" who held prominent positions that require vision frustrated Jesus.

"*Let them alone. They are* **blind leaders** *of the blind. And* **if the blind leads the blind**, *both will fall into a ditch.*"

"*Woe to you,* **blind guides**, *who say, Whoever swears by the temple, it is nothing; but whoever swears by the gold of the temple, he is obliged to perform it.* **Fools and blind!** *For which is greater, the gold or the temple that sanctifies the gold? And, 'Whoever swears by the altar, it is nothing; but whoever swears by the gift that is on it, he is obliged to perform it.* **Fools and blind!** *For which is greater, the gift or the altar that sanctifies the gift? Therefore he who swears by the altar, swears by it and by all things on it. He who swears by the temple, swears by it and by Him who dwells in it. And he who swears by heaven, swears by the throne of God and by Him who sits on it. Woe to you, scribes and Pharisees, hypocrites! For you pay tithe of mint and anise and cummin, and have neglected the weightier matters of the law: justice and mercy and faith. These you ought to have done, without leaving the others undone.* **Blind guides**, *who strain out a gnat and swallow a camel! Woe to you, scribes and Pharisees, hypocrites! For you cleanse the outside of the cup and dish, but inside they are full of extortion and self-indulgence.* **Blind Pharisee**, *first cleanse the inside of the cup and dish, that the outside of them may be clean also.*"

Over and over, again and again, I would constantly hear a voice echo inside of me trying to convince me that even though all men may be good, all good men are not good for me and the vision God has purposed me to fulfill. So, the vision became the force behind all major decisions pertaining to leaders and positional gifts especially, because it demanded conformance-based performance over insignificant performance and activity.

Let's define the two words that carry the weight of Proverbs 29:18 **vision** and **perish**. **Vision** according to Webster is something supernaturally revealed. To paraphrase, it is *a revelation from God* or *a God implanted mental reality that houses the inborn purposes and plans* for an individual, family, church, or nation. It is the future exposed— *spiritually* in the mind today, before it manifests naturally tomorrow. Vision restrains, governs, and guides the operation perimeters of those to be impacted by it like a blueprint or a road map.

Therefore it must be written very plain and simple so everyone involved or to be impacted by it can understand how to purposefully conform their efforts and participation. Notice in Jeremiah 29:11 and Ephesians 2:10 of the Amplified Bible: **To perish** means to be destroyed, ruined, or wiped out. So, if we put these two words together the meaning exposes vision as God's way of birthing, sustaining, and directing the world or an individual to prevent their destruction or ruin.

Even though most of us will spend sufficient time planning entertainment and vacations, far too few of us have considered the need to plan our destiny along with our most precious resources: our gifts and our time.

So what's the point?

- ❖ Do I have a destination in mind for my life?
- ❖ Have I plotted a strategy to get there?
- ❖ How will I know when I hit an important milestone or mark in my life?
- ❖ How will I know when I fall off course without vision or plans?
- ❖ Have I asked myself what I want to accomplish in my life?
- ❖ (Something to remember; most people do not monitor how they "spend" their time. But how you spend it determines what you purchase with it!)
- ❖ Ephesians 5:15 points out that time yields to us whatever we spend it on.
- ❖ What am I purchasing with my time?

Here is what you must decide as you work through this book: If you spend your time on **nothing**, you will have nothing to show for it!

If you spend your time on **wrong things** you will have wrong things to show for it!

If you spend it on **distractions**, you will have distractions to show for it!

But if you spend it on **vision** your future will emerge!

- ❖ Make every minute count! Remember to say to yourself: "I must first see, next plan, and then I must act, if I am going to live a purposeful life."
- ❖ Only action ignites my dreams, plans, and goals into a living force.
- ❖ Procrastination holds me back because of fear and insecurities.
- ❖ To conquer fear I must learn to act without hesitation.
- ❖ To act without hesitation requires strong familiarity with my plan.

What I have learned is that to operate by a God inspired, carefully planned vision is a solution that will affect every area of my life that has become a problem to me. This solution will integrate all the issues of your life into one so you can become the same person at home, work, and with friends. Remember, Jesus came that you might have abundant life.

"Vision-filled Faith and Purposeful Obedience to God's Word"

By now you have heard me repeat many times, "for me the answer was structuring my life to align with the Word of God". This enabled me to always have a **standard** for my actions, a **guide** for directions, and **perimeters** to conform my actions and operations so that what I expect is the thing I manifest.

From this, the Holy Spirit inspired a principle using the acronym "EAM." The "E" is expectation, "A" is application, and the "M" is for manifestation. Everything I expect requires a specific application which ensures manifestation. This is how the integrity of God is affirmed. "He hastens to perform His word or He watches over his word to perform it", not the wrong interpretation of it.

What many lack is a vision or an **internal core** [commitment to the word] that allows you to define yourself, and then express that "defined self" in a way that makes life work for you. As long as you continue to allow yourself to be constantly **controlled by external forces** both your performance and well-being will continue to be severely affected.

Structured priorities affect us internally and externally. They affect the way we experience work and life, our relationships with others, and the degree in which we are successful in all our natural and spiritual pursuits. You must establish an internal core that corresponds with who you are by beginning to think through all of your exchanges relative to your internal core. It is true vision that keeps God at the center of an individual's life and as the primary reason we do what we do.

Your VISION must be TRANSCRIBED so your PURPOSE can be RATIFIED! Vision helps lay aside weight and sin. Through the power of vision my life has been transformed. These principle disciplines have worked together to help me structure and regain the purpose for my existence.

My **VISION** needed TRANSCRIPTION, My **TIME** needed an ASSIGNMENT, My **RELATIONSHIPS** needed DEFINING, My **MONEY** needed a MISSION, My **FAITH** needed a DEFINITE GOAL and a CHIEF AIM, My **CONFESSIONS** needed RESTRICTIONS, My **THOUGHTS** needed to be TRIED, My **EMOTIONS** needed to be WEIGHED.

I learned an important lesson to get my life in order. These are the Four Master keys that I used;

- I corrected my Foundation.
- I took an in depth study of my life 'SELF

DISCOVERY'

- I followed known examples to identify the Power of the Pattern successful individuals used.

- I Prioritized the 3-Part man "Setting your house in Order"

My FOUNDATION needed Correction, My Identity needed Discovery, I needed to Follow Success Examples, and I Set My HOUSE in ORDER.

Chapter 9

The Sixth Master Key

TIME

Impacts your entire Life?

My Time Needs an Assignment!

"*We are to make the very most of our time, buying up each opportunity, because the days are evil. Therefore do not be vague and thoughtless and foolish, but understanding and firmly grasping what the will of the Lord is.*" (Ephesians 5:16, 17)

The word of God makes a great deal out of order and priority. The Holy Spirit revealed to me at a very important time in my life that "when we live without priorities, we live out of order. When we live life out of order our life is in chaos. To avoid chaos we must learn to assign our time wisely and keep our appointments and corresponding commitments.

Paul's instructions to the brethren in Ephesus are specific and urgent, regarding the use of their time. Notice, the emphasis, "*Look **carefully** how you walk! Live **purposefully** and **worthily** and accurately, not as unwise and witless, but as **wise, sensible** and **intelligent, making the very most of your time**, buying up each opportunity, because the days are evil.*"

In other words, maximize the use of every moment each day by wisely using every opportunity and assignment for the advancement of the purpose for which you were created. Indicating that time well spent equals the sure purchasing of a purposeful, worthy, accurate, wise, sensible, and intelligent life. The primary use of your "Time" should correspond with your vision and purpose each day.

He further instructs; *"Do not be vague and thoughtless and foolish, but understanding and firmly grasping what the will of the Lord is."*

This statement reaffirms the emphasis of the King James Version, which uses the phrase **"the circumspect walk."** A phrase that signifies **walking accurately**, and in the right way; in order to consistently walk in the way of God's will and intentional purpose for us. God's will for us, should always be first priority to us, because its' significant inclusion will determine both our life's peace and fulfillment.

"Not as fools", He implies, who strays away from their paths, enticed by all adventures, because they have no understanding of their duty, or the value of their souls. Their constant neglect, mental inactivity, and lack of proper personal maintenance, causes them to fall into sin, and destroy themselves by becoming captive to themselves and the will of Satan.

Clearly a quote from Miles Monroe, adequately describes the devastation of ignorance with regards to the abuse of time: "If you don't know the purpose of a thing, abuse is inevitable."

Time is possibly the single most abused, neglected, misappropriated, and unappreciated resource that all men share. This was certainly my case for many years because I really had no concept of time at all. Although similar to my ignorance of laws and principles that navigate success with money and relationships, I was totally, innocently blind to the laws and principles that govern successful time management.

I actually grew up thinking that it was appropriate to assist as many persons and situations as I possibly could. Hardly ever did I use the word "No." In fact for many years after I married my lovely wife and we were blessed with three beautiful kids. I wasted a lot of time in the streets after work, taking on task that concerned the welfare of others, cheating my family of their lawful needs that I was responsible for fulfilling as a husband and father.

I really thought I was doing what was required of me as a

pastor, duplicating what I saw demonstrated by prominent area Pastors. Looking back, I'm amazed that my heart was able to deceive me into thinking that my duty as a Christian was to take care of everyone else's needs and God would automatically take care of mine.

I had absolutely no idea that I was using and abusing my "time" to violate "the laws of preservations". Even though I was very studious and fervent in prayer and meditation, I was deceived. Whether you call it, self-deceived, satanically-deceived, traditionally or religiously – deceived, or simply, young and dumb; However you wish to describe it, I was deceived.

Not only was I deceived but, the people who benefited from my self-deception, both young and old, let me stay that way; even though in many cases they were aware of the toll it was taking on my family life.

Categorically, I became a product of Paul's description of the zeal of Israel in his letter to the Romans, chapter 10:2-3, "*I bear them witness that they have a zeal and enthusiasm for God, but it is not enlightened and according to correct and vital knowledge. For being ignorant of the righteousness that God ascribes, which makes one acceptable to him in word, thought, and deed, and seeking to establish a righteousness, a means of salvation, of their own, they did not obey or submit themselves to God's righteousness.*"

Looking back in retrospect, I'm amazed at how sincere, zealous, determined, consistently dependable, lovingly kind and liberally generous I was. I just couldn't stand to see people hungry, hurting and without. But I was wrong because I was using precious time to give away much of the financial resources and other blessings, privileges and opportunities that God was trying to extend to the four people I was most responsible for. This statement may come as a surprise to many, but I had to discover that **"Need does not move God, faith does!"**

Need is supposed to be used by those of us who represent

God as an opportunity and a tool to teach, direct, and train others how to trust in "Jehovah God" who will both provide for them and show them the way of securing provisions for themselves. So they can also experience the fulfillment of the promise, "*And I will bless you to be a Blessing*".

And like so many others who have not evaluated their religious (zealous) efforts against correct biblical righteousness, ignorance was slowly destroying me through my misaligned practices and perceived good deeds.

I never will forget the night I arrived home with my family in the car, after an awesome prayer meeting, and Bible study to discover that my lights or electricity was turned off, and I was broke! I mean "bur-r-r-roke!" Now, I'm saying it like this because at that time, even though I was in my twenties, my house note was only three-hundred-fifty dollars monthly. I had no water- bill; (my grocery, gas, and insurances) was less than seven-hundred-fifty dollars monthly combined. My salary at that time was over forty-thousand dollars annually. I did have a savings that I could not access, (probably the only reason it was safe), but otherwise, I was bur-r-r-roke! I was so broke that I couldn't afford the "o" to keep the "br" connected to the "ke", that's br-o-ke!

The problem was that I had taken off a half of my work shift earlier that day to transport someone to the hospital who had several children older than me. When I arrived at their home, I discovered that they did not have gas money, no grocery, nor had their mortgage note been paid, it was a few weeks over due.

Sensitive to the burden and heaviness, I thought God allowed me to discern, I volunteered to give part, but loan the rest of the money so the person would be relieved for surgery.

From this point the details get a little fuzzy, but I do remember arriving home just in time to pick up my wife and kids for Bible study. The first question my wife asked me, as she got in the car, was did you pay the light-bill. My immediate reply was defensive, because I did not want her to know what I had done.

Her last words on the subject were, "I don't know why you are so defensive but I'm just letting you know they (Aiken-Electric) called and said if it's not paid today, the lights will be turned off." I said nothing else but tried to imply, all is well, I'll take care of it tomorrow.

But, I was in for a rude awakening. After returning home from this awesome Bible study, I alluded to earlier. The electricity was off. I went back outside to check the meter only to discover that the color of the tag had been changed without my consent.

I was trapped. I was angry, and I was caught. My wife refused to go with me to ask my parents for a loan to cover my irresponsibility.

So, there I was, the servant of God, whose entire day was spent running errands and providing for someone else in the name of God only to discover, that, God did not provide for my family, in the name of Finace. That really was a costly lesson.

The ride to my parents was long as I turned on the radio to FM 91.7. The teaching program was "Grace to You" featuring, Dr. John Macarthur. The lesson text was taken from 1 Timothy 5:8, "*if anyone does not provide for his own, and especially for those of his household, he has denied the faith and is worst than an unbeliever.*" I had never heard such foolishness all my life, I thought wait a minute; this principle is actually in the Bible!

As I listen to his exposition, the point was clear that I was ignorant of many biblical principles of responsibility. I became deeply convicted and apologetic. My abuses of time, money, and relationships (family) were now evident to the point, it felt like sin. And from that experience till now, my life is subjected to Kingdom principles guided by the Holy Spirit.

I've learned that "*the way of man is not in him, to direct his steps*" apart from the Spirit of God. But, "*the steps of a good man are ordered by the Lord, He lighted his way.*" Therefore, we should "*ponder the path of our feet and let all of our ways be established."* Not only did Hosea 4:6; ring loudly in my hearing, but, the words of Jesus to the Pharisees also ringed loudly. *"You search the scriptures, for in them you think you have eternal life; and these are they which testify of Me"* (John 5:39).

From that time until now, I have dedicated myself to study out Kingdom methods and practices before adopting them as personal practices. "Circumspect walking" is the effect of true wisdom because it enables Kingdom citizens to live and walk daily within the laws of correspondence while buying up every opportunity and maximizing the privilege of grace given to us.

It is also a metaphor taken from merchants and traders who diligently observe and improve the seasons for merchandise and trade. This insight demands that as Kingdom representatives we become great stewards of our time, because each of us is individually considered as a walking economy. **Everything we do in time is a direct response to the principle of "seed time and harvest or sowing and reaping".**

Again, the urgent emphasis of time redemption is to motivate you to buy back or to purchase your time so that you gain or regain ownership of enough of your time, to recover, to convert into, to set free from the control and dominance of evil forces.

If you are like I was before this revelation, you probably did not realize how valuable and significant time really was and still is. It wasn't until I received this revelation that I began to sense how valuable time is, how much I wasted, and how urgently, I needed to buy it (time) back for the Kingdom.

A great portion of my time was being used against me and much of the remaining portion was not being used to assist me. This was bondage and mental anguish for me. I desperately needed to be free. Thank God for the Spirit of Wisdom and revelation that changed my wrong perspective and misappropriation of "time." I wrote this poem to emphasize what time is to me now. I felt inspired to title it "If Time":

If time were a mountain, it'd be Everest,

If time were water, it'd be an Ocean,

If time were a planet, it'd be Jupiter,

If time were a resource, it'd be time!

Clearly, from this perspective, time is to be viewed as one of the three most important, invaluable and precious resources, or privileges God has given man.

Here is a thought that may help you remember the importance of managing your time. "Time will harvest for you whatever you sow it into, or spend it on. Truth is, if you continue to spend it on nothing, you will purchase and have nothing to show for it, regardless of how long you live".

How you chose to spend your time is paramount in determining the quality of life you will live. This is why you must recognize the importance of assigning your time specifically to accomplish your God given priorities. Which are assignments that have the ability to yield gratification in spite of obstacles?

"Time needs an Assignment"

To "assign," means to set apart or mark for a specific purpose. Designate as in an appointment; to appoint specifically, or to allot for something intentionally.

In this case your time should not be assigned by guessing, or assuming, but, by your understanding what the will of the Lord is for you specifically or what your priorities are presently.

This understanding will enable you to rescue as much time as you can from the evil forces and vices of this world. In other words, the Holy Spirit will empower through your yielding to His leadership a strategy to radically redeem or buy back your time from evil practices and worldly vices that you have fallen in bondage to habitually.

This freedom will allow you to see that no-one and no-thing can hold you in bondage, like you do yourself by choices and decisions for spending the most powerful and accessible resources you have, Time!

The Cost of Mistaken Perception

In Matthew's Gospel, chapters 24 and 25, the use and mistaken perception of the value and importance of time is frequently stated as one of the primary reasons that God uses to determine the promotions or demotions of His stewards.

Renowned author Steven Covey, in his book "The Seven Habits of Highly Effective People" points out that "we gain control of time and events by seeing how they relate to our mission. The demands on our time are important or unimportant, urgent or not urgent. Important things serve our mission; unimportant things don't."

When we fail to establish aims or set goals that are related to our personal mission, many times things (unimportant) will seem to be more important that they are. A good example is an untimely or unanticipated phone call. You must develop the ability to not feel pressured to answer calls just because it's your telephone ringing, especially, when it interferes with an important task or project.

"Time Needs Assignment in Business "

Richard Melton, a highly successful, accomplished and well-known businessman eventually learned that effective time management is one of the cornerstones of successful business management. He now explains, "You cannot expect to take control of your life and your business unless you are also firmly in control of your time."

Mr. Melton also asserts that, "Time Management is not something that you should apply only to your work. You should be applying it to all aspects of your life, to achieving your leisure and family and educational goals as well as your business or career goals. Because time is life, the purpose of time management is to turn you into a more effective user of that all-important resource."

Now, I must admit that I do not know Mr. Melton personally, nor have I ever been in his presence. However, I am familiar with many of his well-documented experiences and quotes. Even though, I cannot affirm his beliefs about Christ, one way or another. I can say this; Mr. Melton has certainly stated clearly a truth expressed throughout the pages of "Holy Writ", that "**Time is life**". How we use it certainly determines the quality of life we will experience.

On another note, you must remember that because this most precious resource (time) must be managed by careful analysis, planning, and execution. Whenever you fail to assign your use of it specifically, your deeply rooted problem patterns of time management which may result from, indecision, inability to say no, lack of self-discipline, lack of planning, confusion in priorities, or lack of goals and objectives may resurface to create obstacles to your success.

Even sometimes success without the right application can create the illusion of ease, which may again result in ineffective and non-progressive living. Successful time management or effective management of you as a resource will require intentional focus, strong commitment, and hard work to turn it into an asset of favor.

"Time is an earthly trust that attracts many robbers" and it is TIME for you to realize this if you are going to maximize your purpose.

A method I now use to manage my time effectively was inspired during my devotion. I refer to it as "Time Zones".

"Time Zones "

The Holy Spirit helped me to simplify my daily approach to living by showing me how to separate my time into "Zones" to rank them by importance. Each of these zones is a period allotted for specific assignments to be accomplished.

First and most important is the **"Sacred Zone."** The Second period is the **"Business Zone."** The third period is [R-and-R] **"Rest and Recovery Zone."** The fourth period is the (REL) or **"Recreation, Entertainment, and Leisure Zone."** The fifth and final period I use a day or a series of 2-3 days of the last week of each month as a **"time of reflection."**

The first four foundational periods enable me to be effective from day to day by keeping me focused on my goals and objectives to be accomplished as I assign them.

The fifth period "Reflection" keeps me realistic about my goals/expectations vs. my real accomplishments. During this time I'm usually able to do an **integrity check**, to see if I'm keeping my word or just making promises that sell me short as a liar. This may sound very strong but it's important that as children of God we practice keeping our word because after all we serve a God who *"Hastens to perform his word."*

It is amazing how much time I lose daily by wasting time with distractions and non-essential things without this structured arrangement.

The Sacred and Business Zones together account for the highest of *my time allotted priorities* because they determine the strength and continuity of my spiritual, mental, relational, and economical existence. How well I manage these zones speak directly to the productivity of my Faith, Family, and Business Focus.

Usually, if I fail to stay within the allotted parameters for either of these I get frustrated and lose my focus which greatly impacts my ability to be affective or productive. My "R-and-R" zone is designed for rest and recovery to keep me from burn-out. Often a lack of rest could affect my ability to be effective in many ways. The most difficult zone for me to manage has been my "REL" zone. So I've learned to make this zone a privilege I have to earn by making sure my checks and balances are in place.

Usually either of these three [recreation, entertainment, or relaxation] improperly managed could cost me quality time away from the zones that qualify me for the "*Good life that God prearranged for us to enjoy.*" It's important to remember that God loves and rewards "***Diligence***" and promises that "*the hand of the diligent shall bear rule.*"

I pray that you will continue to read so that the urgency of these "ingredients to structure" might assist you in your commitment to flourish in the Kingdom of God

This ends part one of the two-book series:

Structure: The Master Key to KINGDOM SUCCESS

Look for book two; part two wherever books are sold or online at: www.FBJM.org or email:

F.BushPublishing@FBJM.org

Bibliography

Barklay, William. *Bible Study Series Commentaries.* 2010. (accessed 2010).

Dictionary.com. *Dictionary.com.* 2011. http://www.dictionary.com (accessed April 8, 2011).

Dictionary.com, LLC. http://www.dictionary.com (accessed April 8, 2011).

CPSIA information can be obtained
at www.ICGtesting.com
Printed in the USA
LVOW03*1323171115

462513LV00005BA/6/P